THE *Yellow* TABLE

A Celebration of Everyday Gatherings:

110 SIMPLE & SEASONAL RECIPES

· ·

BY ANNA WATSON CARL

· ·

Food Photography by Signe Birck

STERLING EPICURE
New York

STERLING EPICURE
New York

An Imprint of Sterling Publishing
1166 Avenue of the Americas
New York, NY 10036

This Sterling Epicure edition published in 2015
First published in 2014 by Yellow Table Press

Recipes & food styling by Anna Watson Carl
Food photography by Signe Birck
Additional photos by Eric Ryan Anderson and Nate Poekert
The Yellow Table logo design by Dana Tanamachi-Williams
Book & cover design by Katie King Rumford

ISBN 978-1-4549-1765-6

Distributed in Canada by Sterling Publishing
c/o Canadian Manda Group, 664 Annette Street
Toronto, Ontario, Canada M6S 2C8
Distributed in the United Kingdom by GMC Distribution Services
Castle Place, 166 High Street, Lewes, East Sussex, England BN7 1XU
Distributed in Australia by Capricorn Link (Australia) Pty. Ltd.
P.O. Box 704, Windsor, NSW 2756, Australia

For information about custom editions, special sales, and premium and corporate purchases, please contact Sterling Special Sales
at 800-805-5489 or specialsales@sterlingpublishing.com.

Manufactured in Canada

2 4 6 8 10 9 7 5 3 1

www.sterlingpublishing.com

TO BRANDON:

For selling your recording equipment and drum kit so
we would have room in our apartment for the yellow
table. For not only believing in my crazy dreams, but
for encouraging me to pursue them. For pushing me
to be the best version of myself. I am certain that
this book would never have happened without your
constant love, support, and encouragement. I love you
to the moon and back.

. . . .

TO MOM AND DAD:

For raising me in a home full of love, laughter, and
delicious—daily!—meals around the yellow table.
For teaching me the importance of conversation,
community, and hospitality. And for passing along
the yellow table to me, so that I can carry on its rich
legacy in my own home.

TABLE OF CONTENTS

01 | INTRODUCTION

Something magical happens when you gather people around a table to share a meal. They can be old friends or they can be strangers, but a transformation always occurs. Once phones are stowed away and conversation begins, people actually start seeing each other in a way that rarely happens in our overly distracted lives. They slow down enough to really listen. They enjoy eating for the sake of eating. Ideas are swapped and imaginations inspired. I've witnessed it time and time again: As stories are told and wine is sipped, the layers begin to peel away. Guards go down and connections are formed. It's something I will never tire of seeing.

At the end of the day, we all want to be known. We want to connect, to tell our story, and to have others listen. We want to be accepted for who we are, and to have a safe place to be ourselves. The table, for me, has always been that place. Cooking is deeply important to me, but it's community that I crave. I will happily throw together an impromptu dinner party if it gets people around the table.

THE YELLOW TABLE

My life has always revolved around the table. I grew up eating nearly every meal at a yellow, wooden table that sat in the center of my family's kitchen. My mom bought the mustard-colored table on a whim, back in the mid-seventies, never dreaming that it would one day inspire a blog or a book. Growing up, birthdays and holidays were celebrated around this table and we spent hours upon hours talking about life, telling stories, and laughing. My parents, brother, and sister were always there, but inevitably, a few friends or relatives would also join. And when it wasn't being used for a meal, the table was covered with art projects, games, homework, or books. It was the center of our home—a place where we felt known and loved, where ideas were birthed and topics debated, and where we learned what life was all about.

In 2002, my mom gave me the yellow table as a college graduation present. And in my various apartments in Pittsburgh, Nashville, and NYC, I've carried on the tradition of shared meals and conversation. Over the past 12 years, I've thrown hundreds of gatherings, small and large, around the yellow table. Some were as simple as roast chicken and potatoes, while others were multi-course affairs, with wine pairings and menu cards.

Ten years ago, when I lived in Nashville, I had weekly Tuesday night dinner parties for anywhere between 6 and 20 guests. The yellow table seats 12, but if more

LEFT: 1970s dinner around the yellow table with my parents and both sets of grandparents. **CENTER:** Our everyday gathering spot in my childhood home. **RIGHT:** Celebrating my sixth birthday at the yellow table. (LEFT)
Brunch gathering around the yellow table in our NYC apartment. **PHOTO BY SIGNE BIRCK** (RIGHT)

people came, we'd add a card table and folding chairs, and eat off paper plates if we ran out of real ones. Everyone brought a bottle of wine and a few dollars to chip in for ingredients. Some friends brought musical instruments as well—guitars, banjos, bongos, fiddles, even a didgeridoo—and after dinner, we'd play music and sing until well past midnight. These are nights I'll never, ever forget.

ON FOOD, FRANCE, AND WRITING

I always knew that I wanted to be a writer, though my love for food came a bit later in life. I studied abroad in Paris, for a semester during my junior year of college, and it changed my life. I was mesmerized by the colorful markets, full of fresh produce and cheeses, rustic loaves of bread, bins of spices and olives, whole fish arranged on beds of shaved ice, and chickens hanging upside down by their feet. I had never seen anything like it. I loved the way the French treated each meal as an occasion to be relished—never rushed—with multiple courses and wine. I was exposed to classic French cuisine—the sauces, the soups, the simple salads with homemade vinaigrettes, and the wine-soaked stews—for the first time, and I was hooked. I returned home certain of three things: I must cook, I must write, and I must return to France.

My career, unsurprisingly, has combined these three things. Throughout my senior year of college and the summer after, I worked in restaurant kitchens, trying to gain some basic culinary skills before I planned to attend culinary school. When I moved back home to Nashville in 2002, I started a small catering company called *fête* and, on the side, wrote restaurant reviews for a local paper, all the while saving up so I could move to France. By the next year, I'd made it to Aix-en-Provence, where I spent six months taking language and cooking classes, and then I moved to Paris, to teach English for a year. By 2004, I was back in Nashville, where I taught classes at the Viking Culinary Arts Center, wrote food and entertaining pieces for

The Tennessean, and edited cookbooks for Favorite Recipes Press. Essentially, I was doing everything I wanted to do—cooking, writing, and editing, plus hosting regular dinner parties in my home—but I still had a nagging feeling that there was more.

I decided I wanted to move to NYC, and work for a food magazine, but I knew I needed a culinary degree first. I applied to the *stagiaire* program at Anne Willan's École de Cuisine La Varenne, in Burgundy, France, and was accepted in 2006. I promptly quit my job and moved back to France. After completing the three-month program (two months of intensive work and study at Château du Feÿ, plus a month-long *stage* at a restaurant), I worked for an additional three months as Anne Willan's editorial assistant for her book, *The Country Cooking of France*. Working so closely with Anne was incredible, and probably shaped my career more than any other experience.

THE BLOG

I finally made it to NYC, in March 2007, ready to pursue a career in food journalism. The table, along with all my other stuff, was packed away in storage in Nashville, and I headed north with just a few suitcases, a couple hundred dollars, and big dreams. Way back then, I had the idea to create The Yellow Table blog. It would be a place to keep the table's spirit alive, while it sat in storage, and an outlet for me to share recipes and stories. But life had other plans.

I hit the ground running in Manhattan. I was working as a personal chef, recipe tester, and magazine editor (for the now-defunct *Culture+Travel*), and living in a tiny closet-sized space with a curtain for a door. There was no time for blogging and no space for dinner parties, but I fell madly in love with the city, soaking up every moment of my new, very busy life. But by early 2009, the economy was seriously suffering and I suddenly found myself, like many others, jobless. With less money in the bank and more time on my

hands, I began cooking at home again. It felt really good to be back in the kitchen, and gave me a chance to start building my repertoire of recipes.

By 2010, the economy had calmed down a bit. I also had a new job, had married my husband, Brandon, and was finally able to bring the yellow table to NYC! My mom and I made the 900-mile trip from Nashville to Manhattan, with the table in the back of a U-Haul truck, and then lugged it up six flights of stairs with the help of Brandon and a friend. We celebrated the arrival of the table that November with ten of our dearest friends and a Thanksgiving feast.

Around this time, I returned to the idea of creating a blog, and after months of hard work, The Yellow Table blog finally launched in September 2011, largely due to the encouragement and help of my amazing and incredibly tech-savvy husband, Brandon. He designed and coded the entire website, and even took the initial food photos, while I created the recipes and wrote the posts. It was truly a labor of love.

THE COOKBOOK DREAM

Writing a cookbook has been a dream of mine for more than ten years. Once I launched the blog, I finally had a place to share my recipes, stories, and dinner parties, and to provide inspiration for others to host their own gatherings. Amazingly, people seemed to like the blog and I heard great feedback from readers who tried the recipes. Naturally I started dreaming again about the possibility of writing a cookbook— *The Yellow Table* cookbook.

As I began slowly researching cookbook possibilities in 2012, I realized it would be far harder than I originally thought. Every agent and publisher told me the same thing: To get a book deal, you need to have a huge following. Cookbook contracts go to TV personalities, top restaurant chefs, and bloggers with 100,000+ unique visitors a day. But a medium-size blogger like me? Not a chance. "Grow your numbers and then we'll talk," is what I heard again and again.

YOU CAN MAKE A WISH OR YOU CAN MAKE IT HAPPEN

In August of 2013, I had my 'aha' moment. After years of writing and recipe-testing for magazines like *Food & Wine, Bon Appétit, Real Simple*, and *Martha Stewart Everyday Food*, as well as cooking for private parties and working hard to grow my blog, I still felt no closer to my cookbook dream. Then one day I saw a sign hanging in a shop that hit me like a lightening bolt. It read: "You can make a wish or you can make it happen." Up until that moment, I had been wishing and waiting for the moment where some magical door was going to open for me. It dawned on me for the first time that I could actually *choose* to make my dream happen. What a novel idea!

The wheels immediately started to turn and for the next six months, I committed not only to creating a cookbook, but also to documenting the process. From October 2013 to March 2014, I wrote a 100-day blog series called The Cookbook Diaries, where I shared the ups and downs and (not always pretty) behind-the-scenes moments of the cookbook-creating process. I asked my food photographer friend, Signe Birck, if she'd take the pictures for the book and she instantly agreed. Signe and I had already been collaborating for a few years—both for the blog and other projects—and had always talked about doing a cookbook together. This book would never have happened without her enthusiastic support and incredible talent.

With no publishing advance and little budget, we shot the entire book in my sixth-floor walk-up apartment, relying on natural light and borrowing props and linens from ABC Carpet & Home (a total dream come true!). I hand painted a bunch of plywood from Home Depot to create colored backdrops and every week we rearranged the apartment to create a makeshift photo studio by the window. I cooked and styled the food and Signe shot each dish on rustic wood floor samples borrowed from PID Floors. Having the chance to use these props and wooden panels was fantastic, except for the fact that we had to haul all of it back and forth each week by subway or taxi. This made for some pretty hilarious and stressful moments, especially given it was the snowiest winter we'd had in years! Elise Inman, my incredible intern, was a godsend, helping me lug bag after bag of groceries and props up my 76 stairs. The upside? We all got in great shape!

Along the way, amazing things started to happen. Jean-Luc le Dû, an award-winning sommelier and owner of Le Dû's Wine Shop, heard about the book and offered to create wine pairings. Design superstar Dana Tanamachi-Williams created a gorgeous new logo for The Yellow Table blog (plus one for The Cookbook Diaries series). The uber-talented photographer Eric Ryan Anderson documented several dinner parties, and shot a teaser film for the project. And when I put a request on the blog for recipe testers, I got more than 100 responses, from readers around the world, all wanting to test recipes for me. The book was becoming a community-sourced endeavor, and I was blown away.

Once the book was shot and the recipes written, I made the surprising (to me, at least!) decision to self-publish. Even though I had talked to a few interested publishers, I hadn't found the right fit. And at the end of the day, I really wanted creative control. After putting so much effort into creating the recipes and photos, I wanted to find a designer that could match our aesthetic and who really got the vision of the project. I also knew that finding the right printer was crucial.

I posted a photo on my blog of me holding a sign that said, "Do you want to design my cookbook?" I was shocked by how many talented individuals emailed me, and wanted to be a part of the project. I ended up selecting Katie King Rumford, a phenomenally talented designer, who was living in Mumbai, India, at the time, but coincidentally was about to move to NYC. She had designed a cookbook of her own, as part of her MFA Thesis, and totally got my desire for lots of white space, classic typeface, and an overall clean aesthetic. I also found a U.S.-based printer, Worzalla, that had printed loads of beautiful cookbooks. Then, just as I was looking for an editor, I met Lauren Salkeld through a friend. She, coincidentally, had ten years of experience testing and developing recipes, as well as editing and writing for websites, magazines, and cookbooks. It's incredible to think how organically the book team came together.

KICKSTARTER

Once I gathered the team, I knew I had to figure out a way to pay for the book. Printing costs are high, but I also needed to pay my team, and recoup some of the costs I'd already sunk into testing and shooting all of the recipes! So, I decided to launch a Kickstarter campaign to pre-sell copies of the book, and raise funds for the first printing. I set the number at $50,000, the break-even point for covering all of the costs for the first print run. It seemed impossibly high, but I believed against all odds that I would make the goal.

LAUREN SALKELD   DANA TANAMACHI-WILLIAMS   BRANDON CARL   SIGNE BIRCK   ERIC RYAN ANDERSON

(BELOW) PHOTOS BY ERIC RYAN ANDERSON, PHOTO OF NATE POEKERT BY NATHAN JOHNSON

I knew that meeting our Kickstarter goal would require some unconventional tactics. So, to create some buzz, I decided to go on a month-long, cross-country road trip, throwing a series of collaborative dinner parties with some of my favorite bloggers, designers, and photographers. Each of my co-hosts could then blog about the dinner party, and help to promote my cookbook and my Kickstarter campaign on social media. I started reaching out to people, completely terrified that they would either ignore me or laugh and say no. But once again, I was amazed by the positive response.

I lined up parties in Raleigh (with Megan and Mike Gilger of The Fresh Exchange), Nashville (with Phillip and Dana Nappi of Peter Nappi), New Orleans (with Joy Wilson of Joy the Baker), Austin (with Jeanine Donofrio of Love & Lemons), Dallas (with Sarah Harmeyer of Neighbor's Table), Los Angeles (with Sarah Sherman Samuel of Smitten Studio), and Seattle (with Jenn Elliott Blake of Scout), and kicked off with a party at the yellow table in NYC. Most incredible of all, several national brands agreed to partner with me: Volkswagen lent me a Beetle to drive, Whole Foods Market supplied ingredients and wine for each dinner party, and GoPro provided a video camera to document the trip. It was truly humbling to see so many people get behind my vision of creating community around the table. Every time a door swung open, I thanked God, and kept moving forward, feeling beyond grateful.

The trip was one of the most incredible (and exhausting!) experiences of my life. Each dinner party was totally unique, from the menu to the space to the guest list. Some were small and intimate, some loud and boisterous, and nearly all were outdoors—mosquitoes, rain, and all! I had the privilege of collaborating with some of the most incredible people, and loved watching the magical connections that inevitably happen when people gather around the table. At the end of the six-week campaign, not only did I meet my $50,000 goal, but I exceeded it by nearly $16,000, with a total of 1,083 backers. Wow!

THE POWER OF COLLABORATION

If there's one takeaway from this project, it's this: Don't be afraid to ask for the impossible. If you don't ask, the answer is already no, so what do you have to lose? It's a lie that you can (and should) do it all on your own—it truly takes a village! This cookbook is a testimony to the power of collaboration, and to the Providence that accompanies the pursuit of a dream.

I hope this book inspires you—and not just to get in the kitchen and cook. I hope that it shows you that dreams can, indeed, come true. All you need is some creativity and elbow grease—and the courage to begin.

Anna

NATE POEKERT
Lifestyle Photographer
nathanpoekert.com

ANNA WATSON CARL
Author
theyellowtable.com

JEAN-LUC LE DÛ
Sommelier
leducwines.com

ELISE INMAN
Intern-in-Chief

KATIE KING RUMFORD
Designer & Illustrator
(Book & Cover)
katiekingrumford.com

02 | WINE PAIRING 101

I am thrilled to introduce my friend Jean-Luc Le Dû, a James Beard Award-winning sommelier who has graciously written wine pairings for many of the recipes in this book. We met several years ago through a mutual friend, and have shared many a great meal (and bottle of wine!) together. He is not only a wine expert—he spent nearly ten years as Head Sommelier at Michelin 3-star restaurant Daniel and currently owns and runs Le Dû Wines in Manhattan—but he is truly passionate about expanding peoples' palates, and introducing them to little-known growing regions and grape varieties. All the wines he chose for this book are under $25 (which is helpful for budget-minded people like me!) and can be ordered at leduwines.com.

With no further ado, here's Jean-Luc:

Pairing wine with food is all about nuance. And, just like adding salt and pepper to a dish, you need to achieve the right balance.

Besides the main ingredient of a dish (be it fish, meat, or vegetable), I pay attention to the elements of the sauce, as its composition determines the type of wine to pair. For example, mushrooms will impart a sense of earthiness that can be balanced with a fruity red, while the sweetness of stewed tomatoes pairs well with a bone-dry white. A good pairing can be achieved in more than one way however, and I urge you to taste and try different wines and see for yourself what you like best. My pairings are only a door, an invitation to enjoy wine and food.

Wine's role at the table is to accompany—not overwhelm—and that is why most of the wines in this book are below 14% in alcohol. Most are organic or biodynamic, while some are in keeping with the "natural" wine movement. Does this necessarily make better wine? The verdict is still out on that, but low-alcohol wines certainly offer a truer expression of their respective terroir.

—Jean-Luc Le Dû

....

PRICE RANGE

$	$5 – $12.99
$$	$13 – $19.99
$$$	$20 – $25.00

WHITES

SPARKLING WINES

Champagne
Cava
Prosecco

Enjoy with...
passed canapés,
cheese, light fish
preparations

FRUITY WHITES

Riesling
Chenin Blanc
Viognier

Enjoy with...
Asian-influenced
dishes, citrus-based
dishes

LIVELY WHITES

Sauvignon Blanc
Grüner Veltliner
Pinot Blanc
Pinot Grigio

Enjoy with...
apéritif, light seafood
dishes, salads

FULL-BODIED WHITES

Chardonnay
Roussanne

Enjoy with...
grilled fish, poultry,
most white meat

ROSÉ

Enjoy all the time...
if the temperature rises
above 80 degrees!

REDS

FRUITY REDS

Pinot Noir
Gamay
Barbera

Enjoy with...
grain-based dishes,
roasted chicken,
hearty fish dishes

MEDIUM-BODIED REDS

Merlot
Sangiovese
Tempranillo

Enjoy with...
lamb, veal, light
beef preparations

RICH REDS

Zinfandel
Petite Syrah
Grenache

Enjoy with...
stews, Middle-Eastern
meat recipes

SPICY REDS

Syrah
Cabernet Franc
Blaufrankisch

Enjoy with...
grilled fish, mushroom-
based recipes, hearty
pork dishes

TANNIC REDS

Cabernet Sauvignon
Nebbiolo
Mourvedre

Enjoy with...
grilled red meat,
winter dishes, roast
leg of lamb

ANATOMY OF A SUGGESTED PAIRING

WINE PRODUCER, NAME, VARIETY, REGION, VINTAGE, (PRICE RANGE)

Though wine names may seem confusing, they can generally be broken down into the following elements: wine producer, name of wine, grape variety, region, and vintage. However, there are exceptions. For example, most wines from the New World (USA, Argentina, Australia, etc.) are identified first by their grape name (Cabernet Sauvingon, Pinot Noir, Chardonnay), while most wines from the Old World (except Austria and Germany) are named after the place where they were produced. It is assumed that the place determines the type of wines it produces, and not vice-versa. American wine areas are slowly coming to this conclusion as well, but for now, you'll notice a difference in the way New and Old World wines are labeled.

Country
Production Note(s)
Price

(LEFT) PHOTO BY NATE POEKERT

03 | HOW TO USE THIS BOOK

A NOTE ABOUT COOKING

I'm a cook, not a chef. Though I do cook professionally, I don't run a restaurant, nor do I have any desire to. For me, cooking is less about science and precision, and more about creativity and intuition. It's about feeding people that I love. So even though the recipes in this book have been thoroughly tested, I want you to use them more as guides than exact blueprints. Feel free to experiment and make them your own. Want a little more lemon? Squeeze away. Think basil would taste better than mint? Give it a try! It's all about taste, which is such a personal thing. I don't usually give specific amounts for salt and pepper, for example, because I want you to taste each dish, and season as you go.

Cooking is all about instinct and learning to trust yourself, which, like tackling a new job or becoming a parent, can only happen with time and lots of practice. I hope this book inspires you to get in the kitchen and play. I hope these pages get splattered with olive oil and sprinkled with flour, and that you scribble notes in the margins. I hope you experiment with ingredients you've never cooked before, try out new techniques or tools, and most of all, that you share your culinary successes (and flops!) with family and friends.

NOTES ABOUT THE RECIPES

• **Serves 4:** I developed most of the recipes to feed 4 people, which means they can be halved to serve 2, doubled to serve 8, or even tripled to serve 12. But there are a few exceptions. Pastries like muffins or cakes, which are baked in specific pans, are designed to feed a crowd. The same is true for soups, stews, and casserole dishes like lasagna. Even if you're not cooking for a large group, go ahead and make a big batch—you can have the leftovers for lunch the next day, or freeze any extras to enjoy later.

• **4 – 5 Ounce Servings:** I'm not a big meat-eater, so when I portion out meat or fish, I generally give each person 4 – 5 ounces, rather than the traditional American 8-ounce serving size. I prefer to have smaller portions of meat, and fill out the plate with vegetables, grains, and salads. It ends up being far more economical to cook this way (and I feel better as well).

• **30-Minute Prep:** The prep for each recipe shouldn't take much longer than 30 minutes. My goal is to make gathering around the table not just doable, but also fun, healthy, and delicious. With this in mind, I included recipes that are simple enough to feed a family on a busy weeknight, but also interesting enough to make for a dinner party.

- **Seasonal Items:** Many of the recipes are very seasonal, which means you might not be able to find the ingredients year-round. So enjoy Caprese salad (page 115) and gazpacho (page 82) in the summer, pea-fava purée (page 182) and strawberry-rhubarb crumbles (page 223) in the spring, butternut squash soup (page 44) in the fall, and blood orange salad (page 136) in the winter.

- **For Even Baking:** As a rule of thumb, it's a good idea to bake things in the center of the oven for the most even cooking. When you're using two baking sheets at once, use the middle and the upper (or lower) racks, switching the pans halfway through the baking time. (Of course if you have a convection oven, this doesn't really matter.) In general, know your oven—mine cooks pretty unevenly, so I have to move things around quite a bit.

BASIC GUIDELINES

Here are a few basic guidelines to keep in mind as you start to cook from this book:

- Read each recipe all the way through (preferably twice) before you start cooking.

- Gather all your ingredients and equipment before you start cooking.

- Buy the freshest ingredients available, and when possible, buy local and/or organic.

- Produce should be thoroughly rinsed in cold water and dried.

- Herbs are fresh and—unless specified—leaves only.

- Citrus (lemon, lime, and orange) is freshly squeezed and freshly grated.

- Garlic is fresh, never jarred.

- Salt is fine sea salt and pepper is freshly ground.

MY FOOD PHILOSOPHY

I'm not a nutritionist, so I'm not going to prescribe a healthy eating plan for you. And even though there are quite a few gluten-free, dairy-free, vegan, and vegetarian recipes in this book (indicated by the following symbols), I'm not advocating that any of these ways of eating is the *right* way.

My husband, Brandon, and I tend to eat lots of seasonal vegetables and fruits, (local and organic, when possible), wild fish, and small amounts of humanely raised poultry, beef, pork, and lamb. We try to keep sugar, dairy, and gluten to a minimum, but we don't avoid these things all together. We love desserts and baked goods, but we try to limit them to special occasions. I love shopping at farmers' markets whenever possible and if I didn't live in Manhattan, I'd love to have a garden. Eating locally is far and away the best option for the environment, for your health, and for your taste buds.

⊙ DF / GF / V

⊙ = *Vegetarian*
DF = *Dairy-Free*
GF = *Gluten-Free*
V = *Vegan*

CONVERSION CHART:

1 lemon = 3 tablespoons juice + 1 tablespoon zest
1 lime = 2 tablespoons juice + 1 tablespoon zest
1 orange = 1/3 cup juice + 1 1/2 tablespoons zest

Baby Spinach or Mixed Greens
5 ounces (1 container) = 6 packed cups

Baby Arugula
5 ounces (1 container) = 7 packed cups

Strawberries, hulled and halved
(or quartered if really big)
16 ounces (1 container) = 2 1/2 cups

Garlic
1 clove minced = a little less than 1 teaspoon

Shallot
1 medium minced = about 1/4 cup

THE PANTRY

Having a well-stocked pantry (and refrigerator) makes all the difference in the world when you come home from a long day at work and ask the age-old question: To cook or not to cook? If you have a few key ingredients on hand, you can toss together a simple meal in no time at all, without making a trip to the grocery store.

The following recommendations are staples in my pantry, and things you'll use when cooking from this book. I usually buy basics (flours, oils, spices, vinegars, sugars, nuts, grains, condiments, yogurt, butter, etc.) at Trader Joe's, because it's so affordable. Produce, fish, and meat, I buy elsewhere, shopping as needed throughout the week. We also subscribe to an amazing weekly farm-delivery service called Quinciple, which provides us with locally sourced produce, eggs, cheeses, bread, meat or fish, and other specialty items.

OILS

Canola oil (or vegetable oil)
Extra-virgin olive oil
Sesame oil

VINEGARS

Balsamic vinegar
Red wine vinegar
Sherry vinegar
White balsamic vinegar
White wine vinegar

FLOURS

All-purpose flour (unbleached)
Almond meal (i.e. almond flour)
Gluten-free all-purpose flour
Whole wheat flour

SWEETENERS

Granulated sugar (or natural cane sugar)
Light and dark brown sugar
Pure maple syrup (grade A or B)
Raw honey (wildflower and lavender)

NUTS

Almonds (whole, raw)
Cashews
Hazelnuts
Pecans

Pine nuts
Pistachios
Walnuts

GRAINS

Brown rice
Couscous
Farro
Quinoa (red and white)

CANNED ITEMS

Black beans
Cannellini beans
Chickpeas
Kidney beans
Pinto beans
Tomatoes (whole, peeled, crushed, diced—I love
   San Marzano)

OTHER PANTRY ITEMS

Baking powder
Baking soda
Chicken stock (I use the free-range, organic variety)
Cocoa powder
Dark chocolate (70–85% bars from Valrhona, Lindt,
   or Ghirardelli)
Dried pasta (egg noodles, no-boil lasagna noodles,
   pappardelle, spaghetti)
Garlic (store in a cool, dry place)
Non-stick cooking spray (I like canola oil spray)
Nutella
Old-fashioned rolled oats (gluten-free or regular; not
   quick-cooking)
Onions (white and red)
Panko breadcrumbs
Peppercorns (and grinder)
Pure vanilla extract
Sea salt (fine and coarse—I season dishes with fine
   sea salt while cooking and finish them with coarse
   sea salt)
Semisweet (or bittersweet) chocolate chips
Shallots
Sprouted green lentils
Vegetable stock

SPICES

Allspice
Cayenne
Chili powder

Cinnamon

Cloves

Coriander

Cumin

Ginger

Nutmeg

Old Bay seasoning

Red pepper flakes

Saffron

Turmeric

REFRIGERATOR

Apricot jam

Arugula

Avocados

Butter (salted and unsalted)

Buttermilk

  (You can create your own buttermilk by adding 1
  tablespoon lemon juice or white vinegar to 1 scant
  cup of milk. Let sit for 5–10 minutes and stir.)

Capers

Carrots

Celery

Dark, leafy greens (kale, Swiss chard, baby spinach)

Eggs (large)

Fresh herbs (basil, cilantro, dill, mint, rosemary,
    parsley, thyme)

Greek yogurt

Heavy whipping cream (and/or heavy cream)

Lemons

Milk (organic—2% or whole)

Olives (Kalamata)

Parmesan or Pecorino

  (I buy a large chunk and freshly grate it as needed.)

Soy sauce (low-sodium)

Tahini

Whole grain Dijon mustard

FREEZER

Baguette

Bananas (overripe)

Naan bread

COOKING TOOLS

You don't need every pot, pan, knife, and cooking tool out there to create a great meal. AND you don't even need a big kitchen—mine is just 48 square feet! Here are some of my favorite cooking tools and appliances, and things you'll find useful when cooking from this book.

Chef's Knife: I have both 8-inch and 10-inch chef's knives and I use them every single day. Having a good quality chef's knife is crucial, so invest in one that will last a long time. And make sure to get it professionally sharpened every few months, as there's nothing more dangerous than a dull knife.

Paring Knife: This little guy is used for smaller projects like slicing an apple or some cheese, coring a tomato, or cleaning fruits and vegetables.

Cutting Board(s): I love having a big cutting board so I can easily chop a bunch of ingredients without things falling off the edges. I use a plastic cutting board for raw meat, and a wooden one for vegetables.

Large Pot: A large pot is essential for boiling pasta and making soups or chili. I recommend using a heavy-bottomed version, to prevent foods from burning.

Medium Saucepan: I use this size pan for cooking grains or blanching small quantities of vegetables.

Large Sauté Pan: Similar to a skillet, but with straight sides instead of sloped, a sauté pan is ideal for simmering dishes with extra liquid; it's also great for searing meat.

Large Skillet: Perfect for sautéing garlic, onions, or greens (the sloping sides make it easy to shake the pan) or searing meat. For both the sauté pan and the skillet, invest in a heavy-bottomed pan, so your food will cook evenly. I love All-Clad (stainless steel and aluminum) for everyday sautéing and Lodge (cast iron) for searing meat or making paninis.

Non-Stick Skillet: Great for cooking eggs, fish, or anything you don't want to stick to the pan.

Grill Pan: Since I don't have an outdoor grill, I use my grill pan all the time for burgers, chicken, fish, and vegetables.

Large Enameled Dutch Oven: I love my Le Creuset Dutch oven, one of my first gifts from Brandon. I use this for tagines, stews, and braising large pieces of meat.

Rimmed Baking Sheets: These are invaluable for roasting vegetables or meats that release juices as they cook; the rimmed edge prevents oil or pan juices from dripping into the oven. And of course they're great for cookies, biscotti, and other baked goods. I recommend investing in at least two.

Baking Dish (9 x 13-inch; ceramic and glass)

Muffin Tins (regular and mini): Regular muffin pans can be used both for muffins and cupcakes; the mini pans are perfect for mini frittatas.

Madeleine Tin: This unique pan is used to bake French-style madeleines (or the pumpkin version found in this book).

Loaf pans (regular and mini)

Cake Pans (regular and springform)

Deep Dish Pie Pan (ceramic and glass)

Ramekins (6-ounce): These are great for baked oatmeal, dark chocolate pudding cakes, and mini crumbles.

Food Processor: I use my food processor all the time to make dips, purées, hummus, and tapenades. It's pretty invaluable.

Blender: I use this a lot for smoothies and to purée soups.

Immersion Blender: An easier option for puréeing soup, with less clean-up!

Stand Mixer or Electric Beaters: The baking recipes in this book reference using a stand mixer, but you can certainly use electric beaters instead. I know a stand mixer is quite an investment (though I do love mine).

Mixing and Ingredient Bowls: Medium and large bowls are great for mixing and prep, and for storing scraps while you cook; small ones are helpful for storing small amounts of already-chopped ingredients.

Measuring Cups (dry and liquid): Some people don't realize this, but dry and liquid measurements are not the same. Use measuring cups for flour or grains and a special liquid measuring cup (with a handle and spout) for oil, milk, or water.

Measuring Spoons: These are essential for baking.

Colander: For rinsing and draining vegetables, beans, or pasta.

Microplane: This is the best tool in the world for zesting citrus, grating Parmesan, shaving chocolate, or grating garlic or ginger. (Wash well in between!)

Lemon Squeezer: This tool is amazing because it allows you to quickly juice a lemon (or lime) without any seeds.

Vegetable Peeler: I love using a peeler to quickly peel carrots or to shave Parmesan or asparagus or even radishes. I find the T-shaped models work best.

Tongs: I use these for everything from turning meat to lifting hot items off a pan.

Heat-Proof Spatula: Great for stirring sauces or other hot items, and scraping down the mixer bowl or food processor.

Parchment Paper: My go-to for covering baking sheets while baking cookies or biscotti; for vegetables and meats I normally use aluminum foil.

04 | SUNRISE

ANYTIME

Gluten-Free Blue Cornmeal Waffles | 26

Crunchy Maple-Pecan Granola | 29

Nutella Crêpes | 30

Crustless Quiche Lorraine | 33

Mini Frittatas with Spinach, Goat Cheese & Roasted Tomatoes | 34

Sour Cream-Banana Muffins | 36

Rosemary-Parmesan Biscuits with Fig Jam & Prosciutto | 39

Baked Cinnamon Crunch Oatmeal | 41

Energy-Boosting Green Smoothie | 43

SPRING

Strawberry-Rhubarb Compote | 43

Orange Zest Scones | 44

Roasted Asparagus with Prosciutto & Over-Easy Eggs | 46

SUMMER

Sausage & Heirloom Tomato Breakfast Casserole | 48

FALL/WINTER

Pumpkin-Spice Pancakes | 51

Cranberry-Orange Streusel Bread | 52

GLUTEN-FREE BLUE CORNMEAL WAFFLES

⊙ GF

Makes 6 waffles

I created this recipe when a friend gave me some organic blue cornmeal and I wanted to figure out a way to use it. Turns out it's delicious in waffles, giving them a crisp texture and nutty flavor. Feel free to swap out yellow cornmeal if you can't find blue, and/or regular flour if you're not gluten-intolerant.

3/4 cup organic blue or yellow cornmeal

3/4 cup gluten-free all-purpose flour

1 tablespoon sugar

1/2 teaspoon ground cinnamon

1/4 teaspoon baking powder

1/4 teaspoon baking soda

1/4 teaspoon fine sea salt

1 cup buttermilk

2 large eggs

*2 tablespoons unsalted butter, melted, plus more for
    brushing the griddle and serving*

Greek yogurt, fresh berries, and honey, for serving

Preheat your waffle maker.

In a medium bowl, whisk together the cornmeal, flour, sugar, cinnamon, baking powder, baking soda, and salt.

Pour the buttermilk into a 2-cup liquid measuring cup, add the eggs, and whisk until combined. Add the buttermilk mixture to the cornmeal mixture, along with 2 tablespoons of the melted butter, and whisk until smooth.

Brush your waffle maker with about 1 teaspoon melted butter. Add 1/2 cup of batter, close the lid, and cook until the waffles are crisp and light golden brown, 2–3 minutes. (Depending on your waffle iron, a green light should signal that the waffles are done.) Repeat with the remaining batter, whisking the batter as necessary before adding it to the waffle maker.

Serve the waffles with a dollop of Greek yogurt, fresh berries, and a drizzle of honey.

DO AHEAD: These waffles are best when eaten straight from the waffle iron, but you can keep the first few waffles warm in a 250°F oven while you finish making the rest.

VARIATION: To make this recipe dairy-free, substitute almond, rice, or soy milk for the buttermilk, and vegetable or coconut oil for the butter. If you want to make these totally vegan, use an egg substitute in place of the eggs.

DF / GF / V ◉

CRUNCHY MAPLE-PECAN GRANOLA

Makes about 6 cups

This granola is a staple in our home. The combination of sweet, salty, and crunchy is absolutely addictive. We eat it for breakfast, for snacks (sometimes with dark chocolate added in), and as an ice cream topping. It also makes a perfect hostess gift.

3 cups old-fashioned rolled oats (not quick-cooking)*
1 1/2 cups whole or roughly chopped pecans
*   (or walnuts, almonds, etc.)*
1 cup sunflower seeds
1/2 cup extra-virgin olive oil

1/4 cup pure maple syrup
1/4 cup packed light brown sugar
1 teaspoon ground cinnamon
Coarse sea salt

Preheat the oven to 300°F. Line 2 baking sheets with parchment paper.

In a large bowl, combine the oats, pecans, and sunflower seeds.

In a small bowl, whisk together the olive oil, maple syrup, brown sugar, and cinnamon until smooth. Pour the maple syrup mixture over the oat mixture and stir well to combine. Divide the mixture between the 2 baking sheets, spread with a spatula, and season lightly with salt.

Bake for 15 minutes, and then stir the granola gently. Depending on your oven, you may want to switch the baking sheets at this point to make sure they cook evenly. Bake for another 15 minutes, and then stir again. Continue baking until the granola is golden brown, 3–5 minutes. Place the baking sheets on racks and let sit until the granola is crisp and completely cool.

Store the granola, in an airtight container at room temperature, for up to 2 weeks—though it likely won't last that long!

*Use gluten-free oats if you have a gluten sensitivity.

NUTELLA CRÊPES

Makes about 15–20 crêpes (depending on how thin you make them)

I fell madly in love with Nutella crêpes when I studied abroad in Paris. Luckily, these are fairly easy create at home—all you need is a crêpe pan (or an 8- to 10- inch nonstick skillet), and a thin spatula for flipping. Making pretty crêpes does take a bit of practice, so plan on tossing out your first few attempts. Feel free to serve these with butter, sugar, or jam in lieu of Nutella.

2 large eggs

1 cup whole milk

2 teaspoons pure vanilla extract

1 cup all-purpose flour

2 tablespoons sugar

2 tablespoons melted unsalted butter,
*   plus more for buttering the pan*

1 1/4 cups Nutella

Powdered sugar, berries, and sliced bananas, for serving

Preheat the oven to 225°F.

Place the eggs, milk, vanilla, flour, sugar, 2 tablespoons of the butter, and 1/4 cup of water in a blender and blend until smooth. (If you don't have a blender, in a medium bowl, whisk together the eggs, milk, vanilla, and 1/4 cup water until smooth. Add the flour and sugar and whisk to combine. Whisk in 2 tablespoons of the melted butter.) Pour the batter through a fine-mesh strainer into another bowl. Cover and refrigerate for at least an hour—or overnight—to allow all the air bubbles to settle.

Heat a crêpe pan (or 8- to 10-inch nonstick skillet) over medium-high heat. Swirl about 1 teaspoon of butter in the pan and add about 3 tablespoons of batter, swirling the pan so that the batter evenly and thinly coats the bottom. Cook until lightly browned, about 30 seconds, then use a thin spatula to flip the crêpe. Cook for another 10–15 seconds, then transfer to a plate. Continue cooking the rest of the batter, adding additional butter to the pan every third crêpe or so. Place the crêpes on a baking sheet, cover with aluminum foil, and keep warm in a 225°F oven until ready to serve.

Crêpes taste best when served right out of the pan, so don't let them sit too long in the oven!

To serve, spread each crêpe with about a tablespoon of Nutella, fold in half, and fold in half again. Dust with powdered sugar, sprinkle with fresh berries or sliced bananas if you like, and serve warm.

GF

CRUSTLESS QUICHE LORRAINE

Serves 6 – 8

I love making quiches with crusts, but when you're in a hurry, this version is so much quicker. It's also perfect for your gluten-free guests. Serve this with a big green salad and some fresh berries, or as part of a brunch buffet.

8 slices nitrate-free bacon, chopped

1 small onion, diced

Fine sea salt and freshly ground black pepper

6 large eggs, beaten

1 1/2 cups whole or 2% milk

2 teaspoons fresh thyme leaves

1 cup shredded Gruyère cheese, divided

Preheat the oven to 375°F. Butter a 9- or 10-inch deep-dish ceramic or glass pie dish.

In a large sauté pan, fry the bacon over medium heat until crisp and brown, 5–7 minutes. Remove the bacon to a paper towel-lined plate. Pour off all but 1 tablespoon of the bacon fat, and return the pan to medium heat. Add the onion and sauté, stirring occasionally, until translucent, 3–4 minutes. Season to taste with salt and pepper. Set aside.

In a medium bowl, whisk together the eggs and milk until smooth. Stir in the thyme and season generously with salt and pepper. (I say generously because I always wish I had added more seasoning when I taste the quiche after it's cooked!)

Spread the bacon and onions in the bottom of the pie dish. Sprinkle with 1/2 cup of the Gruyère cheese then carefully pour the custard into the pie dish. Sprinkle with the remaining 1/2 cup Gruyère cheese.

Bake until the filling is puffed up and golden brown, 50–60 minutes. (If you have an uneven oven like I do, you may need to cover the outer edges of the quiche with foil for the last 20 minutes of cooking so it doesn't get overly brown.) Cool on a rack for 15–20 minutes before serving.

DO AHEAD: Sauté the bacon and onions the day before and mix up the egg and milk mixture. Store separately in airtight containers, in the fridge, and assemble in the morning.

MINI FRITTATAS WITH SPINACH, GOAT CHEESE & ROASTED TOMATOES

⊙ GF

Makes 24 mini frittatas

These small bites are the perfect savory addition to a brunch buffet. And—good news—they can be prepped a day in advance, which means extra sleep for the host!

1 cup halved grape tomatoes (a little over 1/2 pint)

2 tablespoons extra-virgin olive oil, divided

Fine sea salt and freshly ground black pepper

1/2 shallot, minced

5 packed cups baby spinach leaves

5 large eggs

1/3 cup whole milk

1/2 cup crumbled* goat cheese (about 2 ounces)

1/4 cup freshly grated Parmesan

Preheat the oven to 425°F. Line a baking sheet with aluminum foil.

Spread the tomatoes on the foil-lined baking sheet, drizzle with 1/2 tablespoon of the olive oil, season to taste with salt and pepper, and toss to combine. Roast until softened, about 15 minutes. Let cool slightly.

Reduce the oven temperature to 375°F. Spray 1 nonstick (24-cup) mini-muffin tin generously with non-stick cooking spray, or use a paper towel to generously grease the cups with canola oil, and arrange on a baking sheet.

In a large sauté pan, heat the remaining 1 1/2 tablespoons olive oil over medium-high heat. Add the shallot and sauté, stirring occasionally, until translucent, 2–3 minutes. Add the spinach and sauté, stirring constantly, until bright green and wilted, about 2 minutes. Season to taste with salt and pepper and then drain in a paper towel-lined colander. Let the spinach cool slightly then use paper towels to squeeze out any excess liquid.

In a medium bowl, whisk together the eggs and milk. Season generously with salt and pepper.

Divide the tomatoes, spinach, and goat cheese evenly among the 24 muffin cups. Using a small liquid measuring cup with a spout, carefully pour the egg mixture over the spinach, tomatoes, and goat cheese, filling each muffin cup until nearly full. Sprinkle the tops of each frittata with Parmesan.

Bake until the tops of the frittatas are golden and puff up like souffles, about 18 minutes. Place the muffin tin on a rack to cool briefly, then run a small knife around the edge of each frittata and remove them from the tin. Serve warm or at room temperature.

DO AHEAD: Roast the tomatoes, sauté the spinach and shallots, crumble the goat cheese, and whisk together the eggs and milk the day before. Store everything separately in airtight containers and finish assembling and baking the morning of the brunch.

*Don't buy pre-crumbled goat cheese—I find that it's too dry. Just buy a 3 ounce log and crumble it yourself (you will have a little left over).

SOUR CREAM-BANANA MUFFINS

Makes 2 dozen muffins

I keep a stash of ripe bananas in the freezer at all times, just in case I want to whip up a batch of my favorite muffins. They're super moist and not too sweet, with pleasant tanginess from the sour cream. These muffins freeze especially well, so I usually serve a dozen and save the rest.

1 cup all-purpose flour

1 cup whole wheat flour

1 teaspoon ground cinnamon

1 teaspoon baking powder

1/2 teaspoon baking soda

1/2 teaspoon fine sea salt

1/2 cup vegetable or canola oil

3/4 cup light brown sugar

1/4 cup granulated sugar

1 1/2 cups mashed overripe bananas
   (about 3 large bananas)

1 cup sour cream

2 teaspoons pure vanilla extract

2 large eggs

1/2 cup chopped walnuts (optional)

Preheat the oven to 350°F. Line 2 standard (12-cup) muffin tins with paper baking cups.

In a large bowl, whisk together the all-purpose flour, whole wheat flour, cinnamon, baking powder, baking soda, and salt.

In a second large bowl, whisk together the oil, brown sugar, and regular sugar until fully combined. Stir in the bananas, sour cream, and vanilla. Add the eggs, 1 at a time, stirring after each addition. Add the flour mixture and stir until combined. Stir in the walnuts, if using. Fill each paper cup 2/3 full.

Bake until golden brown and a toothpick inserted in the center of a muffin comes out clean, about 20 minutes. Cool on a rack for 10 minutes before serving.

Store the muffins, in an airtight container at room temperature, for up to 3 days or freeze in a plastic freezer bag, up to 1 month.

VARIATION: This recipe can also be used to make 1 (9 x 5 x 3-inch) loaf of banana bread. Grease the loaf pan with canola oil and bake for 50 – 60 minutes.

ROSEMARY-PARMESAN BISCUITS WITH FIG JAM & PROSCIUTTO

Makes 16 mini biscuit sandwiches

Having grown up in the South, I am completely obsessed with biscuit sandwiches. These are a more sophisticated, bite-size version, with fig jam and prosciutto sandwiched between rosemary-Parmesan biscuits.

2 cups all-purpose flour

3/4 cup freshly grated Parmesan, divided

1 tablespoon minced fresh rosemary

2 teaspoons baking powder

3/4 teaspoon fine sea salt

1/2 teaspoon freshly ground black pepper

6 tablespoons cold unsalted butter, cut into small cubes

1 cup cold buttermilk, divided

2 tablespoons whole milk

1/2 cup fig jam

8 thin slices prosciutto, cut in half

Preheat the oven to 375°F. Line a baking sheet with parchment paper.

In a large bowl, stir together the flour, 1/2 cup Parmesan, rosemary, baking powder, salt, and pepper. Add the butter, and use your fingers to quickly rub it into the flour mixture until it's full of pea-size lumps. Add 3/4 cup of the buttermilk, and use your fingers or a fork to toss the mixture together until a sticky dough forms. Add the remaining 1/4 cup buttermilk, 1 tablespoon at a time, if your dough is too dry.

Turn the dough out onto a lightly floured surface and sprinkle with flour. Lightly flour your hands and knead the dough (it will be sticky!) a couple of times until it has a consistent texture and color. (Do not overwork the dough—the less you handle it, the more tender the biscuits will be.)

Pat or roll the dough into a (1 1/2-inch-thick) circle. Dip a 1 1/2-inch biscuit cutter in flour and stamp out as many biscuits as possible. Roll the scraps together and stamp out additional biscuits. There should be about 16 biscuits total. Place the biscuits, about 1 inch apart, on the parchment-lined baking sheet. Brush the tops with a little milk and sprinkle with the remaining 1/4 cup Parmesan.

Bake until the biscuits are lightly golden and a toothpick inserted into the middle of a biscuit comes out clean, 12–15 minutes. Cool on a rack for 10 minutes. The biscuits can sit at room temperature several hours before serving.

Cut the biscuits in half horizontally and top each bottom with a dollop of fig jam and 1/2 slice of prosciutto. Place the other biscuit halves on top of the biscuits and serve immediately.

DO AHEAD: These biscuits are best when served the day they are baked, but to save time, you can measure out your ingredients the night before and store them separately, covered, in the refrigerator. Or, place the unbaked biscuits on a baking sheet, cover with plastic wrap, and freeze for 45 minutes to an hour. Once frozen, place in a resealable plastic freezer bag and freeze until you're ready to bake them at a later date. When ready to bake, arrange the frozen biscuits on a baking sheet, brush with milk, sprinkle with Parmesan, and bake as normal, adding a few minutes to the baking time.

GF ◉

BAKED CINNAMON CRUNCH OATMEAL

Serves 4

A cross between cinnamon-sugar French toast and oatmeal, this is absolutely delicious. Feel free to use 1 or 2% milk to lighten this up a bit, and you can swap out the sugar for maple syrup or honey if you prefer.

1 3/4 cups old-fashioned rolled oats
    (not quick-cooking)*
1/3 cup chopped walnuts or pecans
3 tablespoons packed light brown sugar
3/4 teaspoon ground cinnamon
1/4 teaspoon baking powder
1/4 teaspoon fine sea salt
1 3/4 cups whole milk

1 large egg
1 teaspoon pure vanilla extract
1 1/2 tablespoons unsalted butter, melted,
    plus more for drizzling
Maple syrup, blueberries, and sliced bananas,
    for serving

Preheat the oven to 375°F. Butter the insides of 4 (6-ounce) ovenproof ramekins and place on a baking sheet.

In a large bowl, stir together the oats, walnuts or pecans, brown sugar, cinnamon, baking powder, and salt.

In a medium bowl, whisk together the milk, egg, and vanilla. Add to the oat mixture and stir to combine. Carefully divide the oatmeal evenly among the ramekins (it will be liquidy) and drizzle the top of each one with a little melted butter.

Bake until the oat mixture is set and the tops are golden brown, 30–35 minutes. Set on a rack to cool slightly, then serve with a drizzle of maple syrup, blueberries, and sliced bananas.

*Use gluten-free oats if you have a gluten sensitivity.

DF / GF / V ⊚

ENERGY-BOOSTING GREEN SMOOTHIE

Serves 2

I love green juice, but we don't have a juicer, so I started making this green 'smoothie' in my blender. I don't bother peeling the fruits and vegetables because the skins are packed with nutrients. This drink isn't intended to be very sweet, but feel free to play around with the combo of greens and fruit to get the flavor you like.

1/2 cucumber, cut into 1-inch chunks

2 ribs celery, cut into 1-inch chunks

1 ripe pear or 1 Granny Smith apple, cored and
    cut into 1-inch chunks

3 tablespoons freshly squeezed lemon juice
    (1 lemon)

3 packed cups baby kale

1 packed cup baby spinach

1/2 cup fresh flat-leaf parsley leaves

In a high-powered blender, combine the cucumber, celery, pear or apple, and lemon juice and pulse until combined. Add the kale, spinach, parsley, and 1/4 cup water and push down on the mixture with a wooden stick or the end of a wooden spoon. Pulse several times to combine, then blend until smooth, adding a little more water if you want a thinner consistency. Pour into glasses and serve immediately.

DF / GF / V ⊚

STRAWBERRY-RHUBARB COMPOTE

Makes about 2 cups

This compote will keep for up to a week in the refrigerator and it's delicious on everything from Orange Zest Scones (page 44) to Greek yogurt to pound cake. It's not overly sweet, but feel free to cut back on the sugar if you prefer a bit more tartness.

2 cups hulled, sliced strawberries (about 3/4 pound)

2 cups (1/2-inch thick) sliced rhubarb (about 5 medium stalks)

1/4 cup sugar

3 tablespoons freshly squeezed orange juice (1 orange)

In a medium heavy-bottomed saucepan, combine the strawberries, rhubarb, and sugar. Cook over medium heat, stirring, until the mixture is simmering and the sugar is dissolved, 3–5 minutes. Continue simmering until the rhubarb and strawberries are mostly broken down, but with a few chunks remaining, 7–8 minutes. Stir in the orange juice, pour into a heatproof bowl, and cool to room temperature.

Store the compote, in an airtight container in the refrigerator, for up to 1 week.

ORANGE ZEST SCONES

Makes 16 scones

These scones are light and tender, barely sweet, and have the perfect hint of orange. To save time, mix and shape the scones in advance then freeze them for up to 3 months—just pop them in the oven the morning you want to serve them.

2 1/2 cups all-purpose flour

5 tablespoons sugar

1 tablespoon baking powder

1 tablespoon grated orange zest (1 orange)

1/2 teaspoon fine sea salt

6 tablespoons unsalted butter, cut into small cubes, plus more for serving

1 large egg, plus 1 large egg yolk

1 cup heavy cream, plus more for brushing the scones

Turbinado sugar or additional granulated sugar for sprinkling on the scones

Rhubarb-Strawberry Compote (page 43), for serving

Preheat the oven to 400°F. Line two baking sheets with parchment paper.

In a food processor, pulse together the flour, sugar, baking powder, orange zest, and salt. Add the 6 tablespoons of cubed butter and pulse until the mixture resembles a coarse meal. Transfer to a large bowl. (If you don't have a food processor, whisk the dry ingredients together then add the butter and use your fingers to quickly rub it into the flour mixture until only pea-sized lumps remain.)

In a small bowl, whisk together the egg, egg yolk, and 1 cup heavy cream. Add to the flour mixture and stir until just combined.

Turn the dough out onto a lightly floured surface and sprinkle with flour. Lightly flour your hands and knead the dough (it will be sticky!) a couple of times until it has a consistent texture and color. (Do not overwork the dough—the less you handle it, the more tender the scones will be.)

Pat or roll the dough into a 2-inch-thick circle. Dip a 2-inch biscuit cutter in flour and stamp out as many scones as possible. Roll the scraps together and stamp out additional scones. There should be about 16 scones total. Place the scones, about 1 inch apart, on the parchment-lined baking sheets. Brush the tops with a bit of cream and sprinkle with turbinado sugar.

Bake until the scones are lightly golden and a toothpick inserted into the middle of a scone comes out clean, 15–20 minutes. Cool on a rack for 10 minutes. The scones can sit at room temperature several hours before serving.

Serve with butter and Rhubarb-Strawberry Compote (page 43).

DO AHEAD: These scones are best when served the day they are baked, but to save time, you can measure out your ingredients the night before, and store them separately, covered, in the refrigerator. Or, place the unbaked scones on a baking sheet, cover with plastic wrap, and freeze for 45 minutes to an hour. Once frozen, place in a resealable plastic freezer bag, and freeze until you're ready to bake them at a later date. When ready to bake, arrange the frozen scones on a baking sheet, brush with cream, sprinkle with turbinado sugar, and bake as normal, adding a few minutes to the baking time.

VARIATION: Divide the dough into 2 (8-inch) rounds and cut each into 8 triangles for a total of 16 scones.

ROASTED ASPARAGUS WITH PROSCIUTTO & OVER-EASY EGGS

Serves 4

I'll be honest: I don't love eggs for breakfast. But this recipe, inspired by a dish from Epistrophy, one of our favorite neighborhood cafés, is equally delicious for breakfast, lunch, or dinner. Make the eggs while the asparagus is roasting, so everything can be served hot.

1 pound asparagus, woody ends trimmed

3 tablespoons extra-virgin olive oil, divided

Fine sea salt and freshly ground black pepper

4 large eggs

4 thin slices prosciutto

Shaved Parmesan, for serving*

Preheat the oven to 425° F. Line a baking sheet with aluminum foil.

Arrange the asparagus in a single layer on the baking sheet. Drizzle with 2 tablespoons of the olive oil, season to taste with salt and pepper, and use your hands to roll the asparagus, making sure they are evenly coated in the olive oil. Roast until lightly browned and slightly crisp, 18–20 minutes.

About 10 minutes before the asparagus is done, cook the eggs: In a large, nonstick skillet, heat the remaining 1 tablespoon olive oil over medium-high heat. Break the eggs into the skillet and cook until the whites are starting to set, 2–3 minutes. Carefully add 1/4 cup of water to the pan, lower the heat to medium, and simmer until the yolk has set around the edges and the water has evaporated, about 3 minutes. Season to taste with salt and pepper and remove from the heat.

Divide the asparagus among 4 plates, arrange a slice of prosciutto on each pile of asparagus, and top with an egg. Garnish with Parmesan shavings and serve immediately.

*Eliminate the Parmesan to make a dairy-free dish.

SAUSAGE & HEIRLOOM TOMATO BREAKFAST CASSEROLE

Serves 8 – 12

This is the perfect make-ahead summertime brunch dish. You can assemble everything the night before, store it in the refrigerator, and then bake it in the morning. If you want to make this outside tomato season, substitute sliced grape tomatoes or drained jarred sun-dried tomatoes.

1 pound sweet Italian sausage, casings removed

2 shallots, minced

2 cloves garlic, minced

1/4 cup chopped fresh basil leaves, divided

6 medium heirloom tomatoes,
*   preferably in different colors*

8 large eggs

1 cup whole or 2% milk

1 cup half-and-half

2 cups shredded mozzarella (you can use torn, fresh
*   mozzarella if you want), divided*

1/2 teaspoon fine sea salt, or to taste

1/4 teaspoon freshly ground black pepper, or to taste

Preheat the oven to 375°F. Lightly spray a 9 x 13-inch ceramic baking dish with olive oil spray or grease it with a little olive oil.

In a large skillet, cook the sausage over medium-high heat, breaking it up with a wooden spoon, until crumbly and beginning to brown, 5–6 minutes. Add the shallots and garlic and sauté, stirring occasionally, until the sausage is cooked through and the shallots are translucent, 2–3 minutes. Remove from the heat and stir in 2 tablespoons of the basil. Using a slotted spoon, transfer the mixture to a paper towel-lined plate.

Thinly slice the tomatoes, lay them on a paper-towel-lined baking sheet, and let sit for about 10 minutes to remove extra moisture.

In a large mixing bowl, whisk together the eggs, milk, and half-and-half. Stir in 1 cup of mozzarella, along with the salt and pepper.

Sprinkle the sausage mixture in the bottom of the baking dish and pour the egg mixture over it. Carefully arrange the tomato slices on top, making 3 or 4 long rows and alternating colors to create a pretty pattern. Sprinkle the remaining cup of mozzarella, along with the remaining 2 tablespoons of basil on top.

Bake until the top of the casserole is golden brown, about 30 minutes. Cool on a rack for 5–10 minutes before serving, or serve the casserole at room temperature.

DO AHEAD: Make the sausage mixture and the egg mixture the day before. Store separately, in airtight containers in the refrigerator, and then assemble and bake the casserole in the morning. Or, just make the whole thing the night before, bake until almost cooked (about 20–25 minutes), let cool, cover, and refrigerate. The next morning, reheat the casserole until warmed through and lightly browned. Either way saves time and the casserole still tastes great!

VARIATION: Feel free to eliminate the sausage mixture to make a vegetarian casserole. Add the sautéed shallots and garlic (no draining on paper towels required) to the egg mixture then pour it into the casserole. The vegetarian version needs a bit more salt.

PUMPKIN-SPICE PANCAKES

Makes 16 medium pancakes

This is, hands-down, my favorite fall breakfast, especially served with a few slices of bacon. The batter is thicker and fluffier than most, so it doesn't spread out on the pan—use a spoon or spatula to help flatten it out a bit.

1 1/2 cups all-purpose flour

1 cup whole wheat flour

1/4 cup sugar

1 tablespoon, plus 1 teaspoon baking powder

1 teaspoon baking soda

1 teaspoon fine sea salt

2 teaspoons ground cinnamon

1/2 teaspoon ground nutmeg

1/2 teaspoon ground ginger

1/2 teaspoon ground cloves

2 cups buttermilk

1 cup pumpkin purée (not pumpkin pie mix)

2 large eggs

4 tablespoons unsalted butter, melted, plus more for brushing the griddle and serving

Warm maple syrup, for serving

In a medium bowl, whisk together the all-purpose flour, whole wheat flour, sugar, baking powder, baking soda, salt, cinnamon, nutmeg, ginger, and cloves.

In a large bowl, whisk together the buttermilk, pumpkin purée, eggs, and 4 tablespoons of the melted butter until smooth. Add the flour mixture to the pumpkin mixture and whisk until just combined. Let sit for five minutes. The batter will be very thick.

Heat a large nonstick skillet or griddle over medium heat and brush with melted butter. Working in batches, drop 1/3-cupfuls of batter onto the hot skillet or griddle and cook until bubbles stop forming on the surface of the pancakes, about 2 minutes. Flip the pancakes with a heatproof spatula and cook until golden brown on both sides and done in the middle, 2–3 minutes.

Serve the pancakes as soon as they come off the griddle, with butter and warm maple syrup.

DO AHEAD: These pancakes are best when eaten straight from the griddle, but you can keep the first few pancakes warm in a 250°F oven while you finish making the rest.

CRANBERRY-ORANGE STREUSEL BREAD

Makes 3 mini loaves

One of my college roommates used to make a similar bread, and I fell madly in love with it. It's equally irresistible with coffee for breakfast, or with an afternoon cup of tea. Outside of cranberry season, try making this with blueberries.

STREUSEL TOPPING:

1/2 cup finely chopped walnuts

1/4 cup packed light brown sugar

1/2 teaspoon ground cinnamon

CRANBERRY-ORANGE BREAD:

2 cups all-purpose flour

1 1/2 teaspoons baking powder

1/2 teaspoon baking soda

1/2 teaspoon fine sea salt

1/2 teaspoon ground cinnamon

1/4 teaspoon ground nutmeg

1 1/2 cups fresh cranberries, roughly chopped

1 cup granulated sugar

*4 tablespoons (1/2 stick) unsalted butter,
    room temperature*

1 large egg

*1 tablespoon grated orange zest,
    plus 3/4 cup freshly squeezed orange juice
    (3 oranges)*

FOR THE STREUSEL TOPPING:

In a small bowl, toss together the walnuts, brown sugar, and cinnamon.

FOR THE CRANBERRY-ORANGE BREAD:

Preheat the oven to 350°F. Spray 3 mini (5 1/2 x 3 x 2 1/4-inch) loaf pans with non-stick cooking spray or grease with butter or canola oil.

In a large bowl, whisk together the flour, baking powder, baking soda, salt, cinnamon, and nutmeg. Stir in the cranberries.

In the bowl of a stand mixer fitted with the paddle attachment. Beat the butter and granulated sugar on medium speed until light and fluffy, 2–3 minutes. Add the egg and beat until combined. Add the orange zest and juice and beat to incorporate. Reduce the speed to low, and gradually add the flour mixture until just combined. Use a rubber spatula to scrape the batter (it will be thick) into the prepared pans. Sprinkle with the streusel topping.

Bake until the streusel topping is nicely browned and a toothpick inserted in the center of a loaf comes out clean, 35–40 minutes. Cool the pans on a rack for 15 minutes, then turn the loaves out onto the rack. Serve warm or cool completely.

Store the bread, in an airtight container at room temperature, for up to 3 days or wrap in a double layer of plastic and freeze up to 1 month.

VARIATION: This recipe can also be used to make 1 (9 x 5-inch) loaf. Grease the loaf pan with canola oil and bake for 50–60 minutes.

05 | SNACKS

ANYTIME

Smoked Salmon 'Tartare' | 56

Bacon-Wrapped Dates with Almonds | 59

Lettuce Wraps with Tuna & Avocado Poke | 60

Crostini 3 Ways:

Fresh Ricotta with Pea-Mint Pesto | 62

Goat Cheese with Fig-Olive Tapenade | 65

Brie with Sundried Tomato-Walnut Tapenade | 66

Melitzanosalata (Roasted Eggplant Dip) | 69

Citrus-Marinated Olives | 70

Spicy Maple-Rosemary Cocktail Nuts | 73

SUMMER

Crudités with Lemon-Parsley Tahini Dip | 74

Watermelon, Feta & Mint Skewers | 77

WINTER

Baked Spinach & Artichoke Dip | 79

SMOKED SALMON 'TARTARE'

GF

Serves 4

I love salmon tartare, but raw fish isn't for everyone, so I decided to create a smoked salmon version. This is equally elegant served on crackers or in appetizer spoons or endive spears.

4 ounces smoked salmon, finely chopped

1 shallot, finely chopped

2 teaspoons drained capers, finely chopped

1 1/2 teaspoons chopped dill,
*   plus fresh dill sprigs for garnish*

2 teaspoons grated lemon zest, divided (1 lemon)

2 tablespoons freshly squeezed lemon juice,
*   divided (from same lemon)*

1 tablespoon, plus 1 teaspoon extra-virgin olive oil

Fine sea salt and freshly ground black pepper

1/4 cup crème fraîche

Belgian endive spears (optional) or everything crackers
*   (optional) for serving*

In a small bowl, combine the smoked salmon, shallot, capers, chopped dill, 1 teaspoon lemon zest, 1 tablespoon lemon juice, and the olive oil. Season to taste with salt and pepper.

In a second small bowl, whisk together the crème fraîche, the remaining 1 teaspoon lemon zest, and the remaining 1 tablespoon lemon juice. Season to taste with salt and pepper.

Spoon the salmon 'tartare' into individual appetizer spoons or endive spears, or onto everything crackers. Garnish with a dollop (or drizzle) of crème fraîche and a sprig of dill.

DO AHEAD: The smoked salmon tartare and the lemon crème fraîche can both be made in advance and kept in airtight containers in the refrigerator for up to 1 day. In fact, the flavors will actually be better when made in advance.

France
Organic
$19.99

DOMAINE TESTUT, CHABLIS "RIVE DROITE," BURGUNDY, 2012 ($$)

Chardonnay finds bliss when paired with this smoked salmon 'tartare.' Chablis, in Burgundy, makes some of France's driest and most focused Chardonnays. Minerality meets ripeness in this excellent value bottle.

DF / GF

BACON-WRAPPED DATES WITH ALMONDS

Serves 4–6

The hardest thing about bacon-wrapped dates is that you can never make enough. Whenever I serve them at parties, they always disappear immediately! Try blue cheese in place of the almonds for an especially decadent treat.

18 raw unsalted almonds
18 dates
6 slices nitrate-free bacon, cut into thirds

Preheat the oven to 375°F. Line a baking sheet with aluminum foil.

Cut slits in the dates, remove the seeds, and slip almonds into the center of each one. Wrap each date in 1/3 slice of bacon, tucking the loose ends under the date. Arrange the dates in rows on a foil-lined baking sheet.

Bake until the bacon is golden brown and crisp, about 15 minutes. Place on a paper towel-lined plate to soak up some of the grease and let cool slightly before serving. Serve warm or at room temperature.

VALDESPINO, CONTRABANDISTA, MEDIUM DRY AMONTILLADO SHERRY, ANDALUCIA ($$$)

Spain
Fortified
$24.99

Sherry's not your Grandma's tipple anymore. Try a small glass of this off-dry beauty with aromas of butterfingers, figs, and smoky nuts. The warm sweetness enhances the dates and bacon, while the underlying oxidative notes offer a flavor lift.

DF

LETTUCE WRAPS WITH TUNA & AVOCADO POKE

Serves 4

Though I've never been to Hawaii, I love its popular soy- and ginger-spiked raw tuna appetizer. You can serve this dish spooned onto lettuce leaves as pictured, on rice crackers, or in appetizer spoons. The tuna is not cooked, so make sure to buy sashimi-grade quality. To make this into a meal, serve with brown rice on the side.

1 (2-inch) piece fresh ginger, peeled and grated (about 2 tablespoons)

1 shallot, minced

1 jalapeño, seeded and minced (optional)

3 tablespoons finely chopped fresh cilantro leaves

1/4 cup low-sodium soy sauce

2 tablespoons sesame oil

1 pound sashimi-grade tuna, cut into 1/3-inch cubes

1 ripe avocado

Lime wedges, black sesame seeds, and Bibb lettuce leaves (from 1 head), for serving

In a medium bowl, stir together the ginger, shallot, jalapeño (if using), cilantro, soy sauce, and sesame oil. Add the tuna and gently toss. Cover with plastic wrap and refrigerate for 1–2 hours before serving to allow the flavors to combine.

Just before serving, cut the avocado into 1/3-inch cubes. Add it to the tuna mixture, and gently toss.

Separate the lettuce leaves and arrange them on a platter. Spoon poke onto the lettuce leaves, squeeze with lime juice, and sprinkle with black sesame seeds.

Alternatively, arrange the lettuce leaves in a stack, leave the poke in a bowl, and set up a make-your-own buffet—the limes and sesame seeds can be served on the side.

Italy
Organic
$15.99

DRUSIAN, PROSECCO DI VALDOBBIADENE, EXTRA DRY, NV ($$)

To balance the richness of the tuna and avocado, I propose a sparkling wine from Northern Italy. Light-bodied but persistent on the palate, with scents of almond and apple, this wine gives a lift to the recipe.

CROSTINI 3 WAYS:

··

FRESH RICOTTA WITH PEA-MINT PESTO

Serves 4

I love this combination of creamy ricotta, fresh peas, lemon, and mint. It's obviously best to make this in the spring when peas are in season, but you can use good-quality frozen ones the rest of the year.

12 (1/4-inch-thick) baguette slices

2 to 3 tablespoons extra-virgin olive oil,
   plus more for drizzling

1/3 cup fresh shelled peas (about 1/3 pound in the pod)

1 tablespoon coarsely chopped fresh mint leaves,
   plus more for garnish

1/2 clove garlic, minced

2 tablespoons freshly grated Parmesan

1/2 teaspoon grated lemon zest, plus 1 teaspoon freshly
   squeezed lemon juice (1 lemon)

Fine sea salt and freshly ground black pepper

About 1/2 cup fresh ricotta

Preheat the oven to 425°F. Line a baking sheet with aluminum foil.

Arrange the baguette slices on the foil-lined baking sheet and brush 1 side of each with 1 tablespoon of the olive oil. Bake, flipping once, until crisp and golden brown, about 3 minutes per side. Let cool slightly.

Bring a small pot of salted water to a boil, and prepare a bowl of ice water. Add the peas and boil for 1 minute. Drain the peas and plunge them into the bowl of ice water. Let the peas sit in the ice water until cool, then drain them again. Transfer the peas to a food processor. Add the mint, garlic, Parmesan, lemon zest and juice and process until combined, but still chunky. With the machine running, add the remaining 1–2 tablespoons olive oil in a slow, steady stream, blending until the pesto reaches the desired consistency. Season to taste with salt and pepper.

To serve, spread about 1 tablespoon of ricotta on each crostini. Top with a teaspoon or so of pea pesto. Garnish with additional chopped fresh mint and a drizzle of olive oil if desired. Serve immediately.

DO AHEAD: You can make the pea pesto the morning of your gathering. Keep covered in the refrigerator until ready to serve.

SPRITZER, ANYONE?! | *wine + sparkling water*

··

Germany

Organic

$18.99

GEIL, MUSKATELLER TROCKEN, RHEINESSEN, 2013 ($$)

The Spritzer may not be the hippest of drinks, but it happens to be one of the most refreshing apéritifs. The original German version is one half very fragrant Muskateller (think flowers and spices) and one half sparkling water. The result is a light apéritif, perfect for a Spring day. I like the Geil Muskateller Trocken 2013 from Rheinessen.

GOAT CHEESE WITH FIG-OLIVE TAPENADE

Serves 4

This tangy-sweet tapenade, served over goat cheese crostini, is one of my favorite pre-dinner snacks. Use leftover tapenade on sandwiches, roasted pork tenderloin, or grilled chicken.

12 (1/4-inch-thick) baguette slices

3 tablespoons extra-virgin olive oil, divided

1/2 cup (stemmed and halved) dried Calimyrna figs

1/2 cup pitted Kalamata olives

2 teaspoons drained capers

2 teaspoons fresh thyme leaves, plus more for garnish

2 teaspoons balsamic vinegar

Fine sea salt and freshly ground black pepper

1 (3-ounce) log goat cheese

Preheat the oven to 425°F. Line a baking sheet with aluminum foil.

Arrange the baguette slices on the foil-lined baking sheet and brush 1 side of each with the remaining 1 tablespoon olive oil. Bake, flipping once, until crisp and golden brown, about 3 minutes per side. Let cool slightly.

In a food processor, pulse together the figs, olives, capers, and thyme, scraping the sides of the bowl as necessary, until a coarse mixture forms. Add the balsamic vinegar and 2 tablespoons of the olive oil and process until combined. Season to taste with salt and pepper—you won't need much, as this is already so flavorful!

Spread a heaping teaspoon of goat cheese on each crostini and top with a dollop of tapenade. Garnish with additional thyme leaves.

DO AHEAD: The tapenade can be made in advance, and stored in an airtight container in the refrigerator, for up to 5 days. It actually tastes better when made a day ahead.

MOULIN DE GASSAC, "GUILHEM" ROSÉ, PAYS D'HÉRAULT, 2013 ($)

France

Organic

$10.99

This light, aromatic rosé, from the heart of the French Languedoc, frames the crostini's tart goat cheese and intense olive flavors with its fresh, floral notes. Close your eyes, and imagine a window overlooking a field of blooming lavender on a summer day.

BRIE WITH SUNDRIED TOMATO-WALNUT TAPENADE

Serves 4

In addition to being a superb crostini-topper, this sundried tomato tapenade is the perfect condiment to have on-hand since it's extremely versatile. You can serve it with a cheese platter, on sandwiches, with grilled chicken, or tossed with pasta for a last-minute meal.

3 ounces chopped sundried tomatoes
(not the oil-packed kind)
1/4 cup freshly grated Parmesan or Pecorino
1/4 cup fresh flat-leaf parsley leaves,
plus minced parsley for garnish
1/4 cup roughly chopped, toasted walnuts
1 clove garlic, minced

1 shallot, minced
1/4 cup, plus 3 tablespoons extra-virgin olive oil, divided
1 tablespoon white wine vinegar
Fine sea salt and freshly ground black pepper
12 (1/4-inch-thick) baguette slices
12 (2-inch) slices Brie, for serving

Place the sundried tomatoes in a small heatproof bowl and cover with 1 cup of boiling water. Let sit for 10 minutes. Pour through a strainer set over a second small bowl, pressing on the tomatoes to remove any excess liquid; discard the liquid.

Transfer the tomatoes to a food processor, add the Parmesan or Pecorino, parsley, walnuts, garlic, shallot, 3 tablespoons of the olive oil, and the vinegar and pulse to combine. With the machine running, add 3 more tablespoons of the olive oil in a slow, steady stream and continue to pulse until the mixture is blended but still chunky. Season to taste with salt and pepper. Store, in an airtight container in the refrigerator, for up to 5 days. The flavors actually improve when you make this tapenade at least 1 day in advance.

Preheat the oven to 425°F. Line a baking sheet with aluminum foil.

Arrange the baguette slices on the foil-lined baking sheet and brush with the remaining 1 tablespoon olive oil. Bake for 3 minutes, flip, and then top each with a slice of Brie. Bake until the cheese is melted, about 3 minutes. (Alternately, place under the broiler for about 30 seconds.) Top each crostini with 1 teaspoon of tapenade and garnish with minced parsley.

VARIATION: This is also really delicious with goat cheese or fresh ricotta, in lieu of Brie. Bake the crostini 3 minutes per side and spread with cheese afterwards.

DF / GF / V ◉

MELITZANOSALATA (ROASTED EGGPLANT DIP)

Makes about 1 1/2 cups

This dip was inspired by my first few months in NYC. I was staying at an apartment in Astoria, Queens, and pretty much lived off pita and garlicky melitzanosalata from a nearby Greek deli. Whenever I taste this dip, I get nostalgic for that time.

1 large eggplant

1/4 cup freshly squeezed lemon juice (2 lemons)

2 cloves garlic, minced

1 teaspoon ground cumin

1/4 cup extra-virgin olive oil

1/2 cup chopped fresh flat-leaf parsley

Fine sea salt and freshly ground black pepper

Warm whole wheat pita triangles*, for serving

Preheat the oven to 400°F. Line a baking sheet with aluminum foil.

Prick the eggplant all over with a fork and place it on the foil-lined baking sheet. Roast until soft, 30 – 40 minutes. Transfer to a cutting board to cool.

When the eggplant is cool enough to handle, cut it in half and scoop out the flesh; discard the skin.

IF PREPARING BY HAND: Finely chop the eggplant and place it in a bowl. Add the lemon juice, garlic, and cumin and mash together with the back of a fork. Add the olive oil in a slow, steady stream, stirring continuously with a fork, until combined. Stir in the parsley and season to taste with salt and pepper.

IF PREPARING WITH A FOOD PROCESSOR: Place the eggplant in a food processor and add the lemon juice, garlic, and cumin and pulse several times to combine. With the processor running, add the olive oil in a slow, steady stream, blending until the mixture is smooth. Add the parsley and pulse a few times to combine. Season to taste with salt and pepper.

Serve with warm triangles of whole wheat pita bread.

DO AHEAD: Melitzanosalata can be prepared ahead and kept, in an airtight container in the refrigerator, for up to 3 days.

*Eliminate the pita if you have a gluten sensitivity.

CITRUS-MARINATED OLIVES

⊙ DF / GF / V

Serves 4

If I have zero time to prepare an appetizer, marinated olives are my go-to. Just add citrus zest, fresh herbs, red pepper flakes, and a splash of sherry vinaigrette to any combination of olives—preferably not jarred!—and you have the perfect no-fuss party bite.

1 cup mixed olives (with pits)

1 tablespoon extra-virgin olive oil

1 teaspoon sherry vinegar

1/2 tablespoon thinly sliced lemon zest (1 lemon)

1/2 tablespoon thinly sliced orange zest, plus
*   1 tablespoon freshly squeezed orange juice (1 orange)*

1 teaspoon fresh thyme leaves

1 sprig fresh rosemary

1/4 teaspoon red pepper flakes

In a small bowl, stir together the olives, olive oil, sherry vinegar, lemon zest, orange zest and juice, thyme, rosemary leaves, and red pepper flakes; let sit at room temperature for 1 hour so the flavors can mingle.

DO AHEAD: The olives can be made in advance and kept, in an airtight container in the refrigerator, for up to 5 days; stir before serving.

Spain
$15.99

RESZABAL, TXAKOLI, GETARIAKO TXAKOLINA, 2012 ($$)

This wine is zesty, spritzy on the tongue, and imbued with freshness and light saline notes. Light in alcohol (11%), it is simply the perfect apéritif wine.

GF ◉

SPICY MAPLE-ROSEMARY COCKTAIL NUTS

Makes 2 1/2 cups

These insanely tasty cocktail nuts—inspired by a recipe from entertaining guru Ina Garten, aka Barefoot Contessa—are the perfect little something for guests to munch on while you finish cooking. Make sure you stir the nuts as they're cooling, so they don't clump together. Feel free to decrease or increase the amount of cayenne according to your taste buds.

1 cup raw unsalted pecan halves

1/2 cup raw unsalted walnut halves

1/2 cup raw unsalted almonds

1/2 cup raw unsalted cashews

2 tablespoons pure maple syrup

1 tablespoon melted butter (or olive oil)

2 tablespoons finely chopped fresh rosemary

1 tablespoon light brown sugar

1/2 teaspoon cayenne, or more to taste

1 teaspoon coarse sea salt

Preheat the oven to 350°F. Line a baking sheet with parchment paper.

Spread the pecans, walnuts, almonds, and cashews on the parchment-lined baking sheet and roast until light golden brown and fragrant, about 10 minutes.

While the nuts are roasting, in a large bowl, whisk together the maple syrup, butter, rosemary, brown sugar, cayenne, and sea salt. Add the warm nuts and toss to coat.

Dump the nuts back onto the baking sheet and bake for another 10 minutes. Set on a rack until crisp and cool to the touch. Stir every 10 minutes or so, to prevent clumping.

Store, in an airtight container at room temperature, for up to 1 week.

CRUDITÉS WITH LEMON-PARSLEY TAHINI DIP

DF / GF / V

Serves 4

This tangy dip is made with tahini, a sesame paste that's also used to make hummus. I love creating a crudité platter using unexpected vegetables like watermelon radishes, romanesco broccoli, and heirloom carrots—the more colorful, the better! You'll notice that there are not specific amounts for the vegetables in the recipe—just use whatever combination you like.

LEMON-PARSLEY TAHINI DIP:

1/4 cup freshly squeezed lemon juice (2 lemons)

1 clove garlic, minced

1/2 cup fresh flat-leaf parsley leaves

1/4 cup tahini

3 tablespoons extra-virgin olive oil

Fine sea salt and freshly ground black pepper

CRUDITÉS:

Rainbow carrots, halved

Raw snap peas or haricots verts

Romanesco broccoli or cauliflower, cut into florets

Breakfast radishes, halved lengthwise

Watermelon radishes, halved and cut into half-moons

Fennel slices

FOR THE LEMON-PARSLEY TAHINI DIP:

In a small bowl, stir together the lemon juice and garlic and let sit for 2–3 minutes (this takes a bit of the edge off the raw garlic). Transfer to a food processor, add the parsley and tahini, and pulse until the mixture has the consistency of a thick paste. With the motor running, add the olive oil in a slow, steady stream. Add 2 tablespoons of water and blend until completely smooth. Season to taste with salt and pepper.

FOR THE CRUDITÉS:

Arrange the vegetables on a platter and serve with the tahini dip.

DO AHEAD: You can prep the crudités several hours in advance. Place the cut veggies in resealable plastic bags or in airtight containers, cover with moist paper towels, and refrigerate until ready to use. You can make the dip 1 day ahead and store it in an airtight container in the refrigerator.

VARIATION: To make lemon parsley hummus, add 1 (15-ounce) can of chickpeas, rinsed and drained, to the tahini dip in the food processor and pulse to combine. With the motor running, add 2 more tablespoons olive oil and 2 tablespoons water, and blend until smooth. Season to taste with salt and pepper. Store, in an airtight container in the refrigerator, for up to 3 days.

GF ⊙

WATERMELON, FETA & MINT SKEWERS

Serves 4

I've enjoyed this ingredient combination many times in salad form, but I think it's especially cute on toothpicks, and makes a terrific summer appetizer. Make sure to use a firm block of feta so it doesn't crumble when you skewer it.

8 ounces seedless watermelon, cut into 1-inch cubes (about 1 1/2 cups)
2 tablespoons chopped fresh mint leaves
8 ounces French or Greek block feta, cut into 1-inch cubes (about 1 1/2 cups)
Extra-virgin olive oil, for drizzling

In a medium bowl, gently toss the watermelon with the mint. Thread the feta and watermelon onto the toothpicks (I like putting the watermelon on top and the feta on the bottom) then drizzle with olive oil and serve.

DO AHEAD: Cube the watermelon and the feta and store separately, in airtight containers in the refrigerator. An hour or so before serving, toss the watermelon with the mint, assemble the skewers and keep chilled until ready to serve. Drizzle with olive oil just before serving.

DOMAINE SIGALAS, ASSYRTIKO, SANTORINI, 2013 ($$)

Sigalas' volcanic soils, on the island of Santorini, have brought international attention to Greek white wines made from the Assyrtiko grape. Taut and minerally, with bright lime and herbal aromas, Sigalas is assertive enough for the feta, yet delicate in the end.

Greece
Organic
$19.99

BAKED SPINACH & ARTICHOKE DIP

Serves 8

Who doesn't love spinach-artichoke dip? I make mine without mayonnaise—not a fan—but with lots of fresh spinach and garlic, plus four types of cheese.

2 tablespoons extra-virgin olive oil

1 shallot, minced

4 cloves garlic, minced

8 ounces baby spinach (about 10 cups)

Fine sea salt and freshly ground black pepper

1 1/2 cups shredded Italian 4-cheese blend
    (Parmesan, Asiago, Fontina, and Provolone)*

1 (8-ounce) package cream cheese, room temperature

1/2 cup sour cream

1 (14-ounce) can artichoke hearts (not marinated),
    drained and roughly chopped

1/4 – 1/2 teaspoon red pepper flakes

Crostini, crackers, or pita chips, for serving

Preheat the oven to 350°F

In a large skillet, heat the olive oil over medium-high heat. Add the shallot and sauté, stirring occasionally, until translucent, 2–3 minutes. Add the garlic and sauté, stirring occasionally, until fragrant, about 1 minute. Add the spinach gradually and sauté, stirring occasionally, until wilted, about 3 minutes. Season to taste with salt and pepper. Transfer to a colander set in the sink and let drain, pushing down on the spinach with a spoon to remove any excess liquid.

In a large bowl, combine 1 cup of the shredded cheese with the cream cheese, sour cream, artichoke hearts, and red pepper flakes. Add the spinach, stir to combine, and season to taste with salt and pepper.

Spoon the mixture into a 1-quart ovenproof casserole dish and sprinkle with the remaining 1/2 cup shredded cheese.

Bake until bubbly, 25–30 minutes. After baking, I like to put the dip under the broiler on high for 1–2 minutes to brown the top. Be careful not to do it any longer, or your dish could break!

Serve warm with crostini, crackers, or pita chips.

DO AHEAD: This can be assembled in advance, covered, and chilled. Bake as the recipe indicates, but keep it mind that it may need a few extra minutes.

*Trader Joe's carries a Quattro Formaggio blend of cheeses that is great in this recipe. Otherwise, I use a mixture of shredded mozzarella and grated Parmesan.

TABLAS CREEK, "CÔTES DE TABLAS," PASO ROBLES, 2012 ($$$)

For this flavor-packed dish, you want a wine with some oomph! Tablas Creek, near Paso Robles, California, makes this full-bodied, floral, Rhône-style wine. Despite the wine's weight, it delivers a fresh finish.

USA
Biodynamic
$24.99

06 | SOUPS & STEWS

SUMMER

Heirloom Tomato Gazpacho with Mango & Cucumber | 82

FALL/WINTER

Homemade Chicken Noodle Soup with Spinach | 85

Tuscan White Bean Soup with Swiss Chard | 86

Roasted Tomato-Basil Soup | 88

Potato Leek Soup | 91

Spicy Black Bean Soup | 92

Butternut Squash Soup with Spiced Pears | 94

Spicy Seafood Stew | 97

Three-Bean Turkey Chili | 98

Hearty Sprouted Lentil Stew with Kale | 101

Tomato-Chickpea Curry with Kale | 102

Lamb Tagine with Apricots & Figs | 105

HEIRLOOM TOMATO GAZPACHO WITH MANGO & CUCUMBER

DF / GF / V

Serves 4

When it's steamy hot outside, there's nothing I love more than a bowl of cool gazpacho. I think peeling tomatoes is too fussy, so I purée them with the skins on and strain the mixture afterwards. The mango garnish adds a nice hint of sweetness.

1 large English cucumber

2 1/2 pounds ripe red heirloom tomatoes, cored and cut into chunks (juices reserved)

1/4 small red onion, finely chopped, divided

2 cloves garlic, minced

1/4 cup, plus 2 tablespoons fresh cilantro, divided

1/4 cup extra-virgin olive oil, plus more for drizzling

2 tablespoons red wine vinegar

Fine sea salt and freshly ground black pepper

1/2 cup halved yellow and red cherry tomatoes

1/4 cup finely diced mango

Cut off 1/4 of the cucumber and finely chop that portion; reserve for garnish.

Peel the remaining 3/4 cucumber, then cut it in half and scrape out the seeds. Cut the cucumber into chunks and place in a large bowl. Add the large red heirloom tomatoes and their juices, 2 tablespoons of the red onion, the garlic, 1/4 cup of the cilantro, red wine vinegar, and olive oil and stir to combine. Season generously with salt and pepper.

Transfer the soup in batches to a blender and purée until smooth. Pour the soup through a fine-mesh strainer into a bowl. Taste and adjust the seasoning as necessary (I usually find it needs more salt). Cover the gazpacho, and refrigerate until chilled, at least 2 hours.

Serve in bowls, garnished with the remaining cucumber, red onion, and cilantro, along with the red and yellow cherry tomatoes, mango, and a drizzle of olive oil.

Store the gazpacho, in an airtight container in the refrigerator, for up to 1 day.

DF

HOMEMADE CHICKEN NOODLE SOUP WITH SPINACH

Serves 4, with leftovers

I make a pot of this whenever I feel a cold coming on. In addition to the traditional carrot, celery, and onion, I love adding lots of fresh spinach. If you happen to have homemade chicken stock in your freezer, this is a good time to use it.

2–3 tablespoons extra-virgin olive oil

2 medium carrots, peeled and diced

2 ribs celery, diced

1/2 medium white or yellow onion, diced

2 cloves garlic, minced

1 1/2 teaspoons fresh thyme leaves

Fine sea salt and freshly ground black pepper

3 quarts organic chicken stock, homemade or store-bought

8 ounces dried wide egg noodles

1 1/2 cups shredded, cooked, organic chicken
   (can be white or dark meat and roasted, poached, or store-bought rotisserie)

4 packed cups baby spinach leaves

In a large heavy-bottomed pot, heat the olive oil over medium-high heat. Add the carrots, celery, and onion and sauté, stirring occasionally, until the vegetables are soft and the onion is translucent, 3–4 minutes. Add the garlic and thyme and sauté, stirring occasionally, until fragrant, about 1 minute. Season to taste with salt and pepper. Add the chicken stock and bring to a boil. Add the egg noodles, reduce the heat to low and simmer, partially covered until the noodles have softened a bit, about 5 minutes. Stir in the chicken and the spinach and simmer until the chicken is heated through and the noodles are fully cooked, 2–3 minutes. Season generously with salt and pepper.

TUSCAN WHITE BEAN SOUP WITH SWISS CHARD

Serves 4, with leftovers

In winter, this soup is on weekly rotation at our house. It's both healthy and satisfying, and it keeps for several days in the refrigerator. The secret ingredient? Parmesan rind—keep a few in the freezer to have on hand for soup-making.

2 tablespoons extra-virgin olive oil

1 medium onion, diced

2 ribs celery, diced

2 medium carrots, peeled and diced

3 cloves garlic, minced

4 slices prosciutto, finely chopped

1 tablespoon chopped fresh rosemary, divided

1 tablespoon fresh thyme leaves, divided

1/2 teaspoon red pepper flakes (optional)

1 bay leaf

3 (15-ounce) cans cannellini beans, rinsed and drained

4 cups chicken stock

1 Parmesan rind

1 bunch Swiss chard, kale, or spinach, stems removed, cut into bite size pieces

1 teaspoon balsamic vinegar

Fine sea salt and freshly ground black pepper

Freshly grated Parmesan and warm crusty bread, for serving (optional)

In a large heavy-bottomed pot, heat the oil over medium-high heat. Add the onion, celery, and carrots and sauté, stirring occasionally, until the vegetables are soft and the onion is translucent, 3–4 minutes. Add the garlic and sauté, stirring occasionally, until fragrant, about 1 minute. Add the prosciutto, 1/2 tablespoon rosemary, 1/2 tablespoon thyme, the red pepper flakes, if using, and the bay leaf and sauté, stirring occasionally, until the prosciutto is beginning to brown, about 3 minutes. Stir in the beans and cook for 1–2 minutes. Add the chicken stock, toss in the Parmesan rind, and bring to a boil. Reduce the heat to low, cover partially, and simmer, stirring occasionally, until thickened, about 30 minutes.

Add the Swiss chard, kale, or spinach, and simmer, stirring occasionally, until wilted, 2–3 minutes. Add the remaining 1/2 tablespoon rosemary and the remaining 1/2 tablespoon thyme, along with the balsamic vinegar. Season to taste with salt and pepper. Remove the Parmesan rind and the bay leaf (if you can find them!) before serving.

Serve with grated Parmesan cheese and warm crusty bread.

Store the soup, in an airtight container in the refrigerator, for up to 3 days, or in the freezer, for up to 3 months. When reheating leftovers, you may need to add a little water, because this soup gets thicker the longer it sits.

ROASTED TOMATO-BASIL SOUP

⊙ GF

Serves 4, with leftovers | Serve with The Best Grilled Cheese Sandwiches (page 162)

Tomato basil soup is one of my ultimate comfort foods. My take is ever-so-slightly sweet, with a richness that comes from roasting the tomatoes before puréeing them.

2 pounds Roma tomatoes, quartered

4 tablespoons extra-virgin olive oil, divided

Fine sea salt and freshly ground black pepper

1 small red onion, minced

3 cloves garlic, minced

1 (28-ounce) can crushed tomatoes

*1/2 cup chopped fresh basil leaves, divided,
    plus finely sliced basil for serving*

2 tablespoons sugar

Pinch red pepper flakes (optional)

*1/4 cup, plus 2 tablespoons heavy cream
    (or half-and-half)*

Preheat the oven to 425°F. Line a baking sheet with aluminum foil.

Arrange the tomatoes, cut side up, on the baking sheet, and drizzle with 2 tablespoons of the olive oil. Season to taste with salt and pepper. Roast until softened and beginning to brown, 35–40 minutes. Cool slightly.

In a large heavy-bottomed pot, heat the remaining 2 tablespoons olive oil over medium-high heat. Add the red onion and sauté, stirring occasionally, until translucent, 3–4 minutes. Add the garlic and sauté until fragrant, stirring occasionally, about 1 minute. Add the roasted tomatoes, canned crushed tomatoes, 1/4 cup of the basil, the sugar, and 3 cups water. If you want a little bit of a kick, stir in a pinch of red pepper flakes. Season to taste with salt and pepper. Bring the soup to a boil, then reduce the heat to low and simmer, partially covered, until thickened, about 30 minutes. Stir in the remaining 1/4 cup basil.

Transfer the soup in batches to a blender and purée until smooth. (NOTE: Be careful of the hot liquid! Make sure to hold down the lid with a thick towel so you don't get burned.) Feel free to thin the soup with additional water if it appears too thick. Pour back into a clean pot to keep warm on the stove. Stir in the cream, and season to taste with salt and pepper.

Serve in bowls and garnish with finely sliced basil.

Store the soup, in an airtight container in the refrigerator, for up to 2 days or in the freezer, for up to 3 months.

GF ◉

POTATO LEEK SOUP

Serves 4, with leftovers | Serve with Arugula, Radicchio & Fennel Salad (page 132)

I used to make this soup a lot when I lived in France. It's just so simple and satisfying. Add a big salad and a crusty baguette and you have the perfect weeknight supper.

3 large leeks

2 tablespoons extra-virgin olive oil

Fine sea salt and freshly ground black pepper

4 medium Yukon Gold potatoes (about 2 pounds total), peeled and cut into 1/2-inch pieces

4 cups vegetable stock

6 fresh thyme sprigs plus 1 teaspoon fresh thyme leaves

1/4 cup heavy (or light) cream

1/2 cup chopped fresh flat-leaf parsley leaves, plus 4 sprigs for garnish

Crème fraîche (or Greek yogurt) for garnish

Crusty bread, for serving (optional)

Cut the leeks in half lengthwise, rinse well, and thinly slice the white and light green portions; discard the rest.

In a large heavy-bottomed pot, heat the olive oil over medium-high heat. Add the leeks and sauté, stirring occasionally, until softened and beginning to brown, about 10 minutes. Season to taste with salt and pepper. Add the potatoes, vegetable stock, thyme sprigs and 1 cup water and bring to a boil. Reduce the heat to low and simmer, partially covered, until the potatoes are softened, about 25 minutes. Remove from the heat and pull out the thyme sprigs.

Transfer the soup in batches to a blender and purée until smooth. (NOTE: Be careful of the hot liquid!! Make sure to hold down the lid with a thick towel so you don't get burned!) Pour back into a clean pot and stir in the cream, along with the thyme leaves and parsley. Season generously with salt and pepper.

Serve in bowls, garnished with a dollop of crème fraîche and a parsley sprig. Serve hot with crusty bread for a perfect winter day treat!

Store the soup, in an airtight container in the refrigerator, up to 3 days, or in the freezer, for up to 3 months.

SPICY BLACK BEAN SOUP

DF / GF / V

Serves 4, with leftovers | Serve with Detox Kale Salad (page 127)

Another standby at my house, this spicy vegan soup takes just 30 minutes to make. It freezes really well, so double the recipe and save half for a rainy (or snowy!) day.

2 tablespoons extra-virgin olive oil

1 small red onion, finely chopped

4 cloves garlic, minced

1 jalapeño, seeded and minced (optional)

2 teaspoons ground cumin

1/2 teaspoon ground coriander

1/4 teaspoon cayenne

3 (15-ounce) cans black beans, rinsed and drained

3 – 4 cups vegetable stock

1/2 cup chopped fresh cilantro, divided, plus a few sprigs for garnish

2 tablespoons freshly squeezed lime juice (1 lime)

Fine sea salt and freshly ground black pepper

Greek yogurt, for garnish (optional)

In a large heavy-bottomed pot, heat the olive oil over medium-high heat. Add the onion and sauté, stirring occasionally, until translucent, 3–4 minutes. Add the garlic and jalapeño, if using, and sauté, stirring occasionally, until fragrant, about 1 minute. Add the cumin, coriander, and cayenne and sauté, stirring constantly until fragrant, about 2 minutes. Stir in the black beans, then add about 3 cups of the vegetable stock (enough to just cover the beans) and bring to a boil. Stir in 1/4 cup of the chopped cilantro, reduce the heat to low, and simmer, stirring occasionally, until thickened, about 15 minutes. Stir in additional broth if you want a thinner consistency. (If you want a thicker consistency, use an immersion blender to purée the soup partially or fully.) Add the lime juice, along with the remaining 1/4 cup chopped cilantro, and season to taste with salt and pepper.

Serve in bowls with a dollop of Greek yogurt (if using) and a sprig of cilantro.

DO AHEAD: This soup can be made ahead, and kept in an airtight container in the refrigerator for 3 days, or frozen for up to 3 months.

BUTTERNUT SQUASH SOUP WITH SPICED PEARS

Serves 4, with leftovers | Serve with Arugula, Radicchio & Fennel Salad (page 132)

I first tried this soup at a Newfoundland-themed dinner at the James Beard House in downtown Manhattan, and was determined to recreate it at home. I love the combination of pears and butternut squash, and the way they create such a creamy texture without any cream.

FOR THE BUTTERNUT SQUASH SOUP:

3 cups peeled, cubed butternut squash (about 1 pound)

1/2 medium yellow onion, halved and thinly sliced

1 carrot, peeled and diced

2 tablespoons extra-virgin olive oil

Fine sea salt and freshly ground black pepper

6 sprigs fresh thyme, divided

2 cloves garlic, minced

2 tablespoons packed light brown sugar

1 teaspoon ground cinnamon

1 teaspoon ground nutmeg

1/2 teaspoon ground ginger

1/2 teaspoon ground coriander

4 cups vegetable stock

FOR THE SPICED PEARS:

1 tablespoon extra-virgin olive oil

2 Bosc pears, peeled, cored, and cut into small cubes

1/2 teaspoon ground cinnamon

1/4 teaspoon curry powder

1/4 teaspoon ground cloves

1/4 teaspoon ground cumin

Crème fraîche or Greek yogurt, for serving (optional)

FOR THE BUTTERNUT SQUASH SOUP:

Preheat the oven to 425°F. Line a baking sheet with aluminum foil.

Place the squash, onions, and carrot on the foil-lined baking sheet. Drizzle with the olive oil, season to taste with salt and pepper, and toss to combine. Scatter 4 thyme sprigs on top of the vegetables. Roast until tender, about 30 minutes. Discard the thyme sprigs.

Transfer the squash mixture to a large heavy-bottomed pot, add the garlic, brown sugar, cinnamon, nutmeg, ginger, and coriander and stir to combine. Place the pot over medium-high heat and cook for 2 minutes. Add the vegetable stock and the remaining 2 thyme sprigs and bring to a boil. Reduce the heat to low and simmer, covered, until the squash is nearly falling apart, about 10 minutes. Remove from the heat and let cool slightly. Discard the thyme sprigs.

FOR THE SPICED PEARS:

In a large skillet, heat the olive oil over medium-high heat. Add the pears and sauté until tender, about 2 minutes. Add the cinnamon, curry powder, cloves, and cumin and sauté, stirring occasionally, until the pears are tender and coated in the spices, about 3 minutes. Set aside.

You have two options here. Either transfer the soup and the pears in batches to a blender and purée until smooth. (NOTE: Be careful of the hot liquid!! Make sure to hold down the lid with a thick towel so you don't get burned.) Feel free to thin the soup with additional broth if it appears too thick. Pour back into a clean pot to keep warm on the stove. Season to taste with salt and pepper. Or, purée just the soup, and stir in the spiced pears when serving.

Serve in bowls and garnish with a dollop of crème fraîche or Greek yogurt, if desired.

Store the soup, in an airtight container in the refrigerator, for up to 3 days, or in the freezer for up to 3 months.

DF / GF

SPICY SEAFOOD STEW

Serves 4 – 6 | Serve with Citrus Salad with Arugula & Ricotta Salata (page 136)

This is an impressive dinner party dish that's actually a lot easier than it looks. Make the tomato base earlier in the day and keep it in the fridge, then just before serving, reheat the soup, add the seafood, and serve garnished with fennel fronds.

2 tablespoons extra-virgin olive oil, plus more for drizzling

1 large bulb fennel, thinly sliced (fronds saved for garnish)

3 cloves garlic, chopped

1/2 cup dry white wine

1 (28-ounce) can whole peeled tomatoes and their juices

3 cups chicken (or seafood) stock

1 teaspoon saffron threads

10 – 12 ounces firm-fleshed white fish, such as cod or halibut, cut into bite-size pieces

1/2 pound medium shrimp (about 20), peeled and deveined

1 pound mussels (about 24), cleaned and debearded

2 teaspoons grated orange zest (1 medium orange)

1/2 cup chopped fresh flat-leaf parsley leaves

1/2 teaspoon red pepper flakes, or more to taste

Fine sea salt and freshly ground black pepper

Crusty bread, for serving

In a large heavy-bottomed pot or Dutch oven, heat the olive oil over medium-high heat. Add the fennel and sauté, stirring occasionally, until beginning to soften, 5 - 7 minutes. Add the garlic and sauté, stirring occasionally, until fragrant, about 1 minute. Add the white wine and cook, stirring frequently, until nearly evaporated, about 3 minutes.

In a medium bowl, use your hands to crush the tomatoes. Add the tomatoes and their juice to the pot, along with the stock and saffron, and bring to a boil. Reduce the heat to low and simmer, partially covered, for 15 minutes. Add the fish, shrimp, and mussels and simmer until the fish is opaque, about 3 minutes. Remove from the heat and let the soup sit until the mussels have opened and the fish is cooked through, about 5 minutes. Remove any mussels that have not opened. Stir in the orange zest, parsley, and red pepper flakes, if using. Season to taste with salt and pepper.

Serve in big bowls, drizzled with olive oil and garnished with fennel fronds, with warm, crusty bread.

THREE-BEAN TURKEY CHILI

Serves 4, with leftovers | *Serve with Shaved Brussels Sprout & Endive Salad (page 142)*

I created this chili as a way to use up leftover Thanksgiving turkey, but it's equally delicious made with roasted chicken. I think it makes the perfect dish for a Sunday afternoon football-watching gathering or a casual Friday night dinner party.

2 – 3 tablespoons extra-virgin olive oil

1 large white or yellow onion, finely chopped

4 cloves garlic, minced

2 tablespoons chili powder

1 tablespoon ground cumin

1 teaspoon dried oregano

1/2 teaspoon cayenne (optional)

1 (28-ounce) can whole peeled tomatoes with their juices

1 (15-ounce) can pinto beans, rinsed and drained

1 (15-ounce) can cannellini beans, rinsed and drained

1 (15-ounce) can kidney beans, rinsed and drained

Fine sea salt and freshly ground black pepper

1 1/2 – 2 cups shredded or chopped roasted turkey

1/3 cup chopped fresh cilantro leaves

Diced avocados, sour cream, shredded cheddar, and crushed tortilla chips, for serving

In a large heavy-bottomed pot, heat the olive oil over medium-high heat. Add the onion and sauté, stirring occasionally, until translucent, 3 – 4 minutes. Add the garlic and sauté, stirring occasionally, until fragrant, about 1 minute. Add the chili powder, cumin, oregano, and cayenne and sauté, stirring constantly, until fragrant, about 2 minutes. Add the tomatoes and their juices, crushing the whole tomatoes gently with a wooden spoon. Add the pinto, cannellini, and kidney beans and 2 1/2 cups water and bring to a boil. Season to taste with salt and pepper. Reduce the heat to low and simmer, stirring occasionally, until thickened, 15 – 20 minutes. Remove from the heat, stir in the turkey and let sit, covered, for several minutes to heat through. Stir in the cilantro and season to taste with salt and pepper.

Serve in bowls, and top with diced avocados, sour cream, shredded cheddar, crushed tortilla chips, or any combination of toppings.

DO AHEAD: This chili can be made ahead, and kept in an airtight container in the refrigerator for 3 days, or frozen for up to 3 months.

VARIATION: You can substitute roasted turkey for roasted chicken, or eliminate the turkey all together for vegan chili.

DF / GF / V ◉

HEARTY SPROUTED LENTIL STEW WITH KALE

Serves 4, with leftovers

This soup is one of my healthy winter standbys. Sprouted lentils are not only more nutritious than the regular variety, but they also cook in about half the time. Feel free to swap out the Tuscan kale for another variety—or use any leafy green like Swiss chard, spinach, or collards.

3 tablespoons extra-virgin olive oil

1 small white or yellow onion, diced

2 medium carrots, peeled and diced

2 ribs celery, diced

2 cloves garlic, minced

1 teaspoon ground cumin

1/2 teaspoon ground coriander

1/4 teaspoon red pepper flakes (optional)

Fine sea salt and freshly ground black pepper

4 cups vegetable stock

1 (14.5-ounce) can diced tomatoes with their juices

1 (10-ounce) package sprouted green lentils*

1 bunch Tuscan (Lacinato) kale, tough stems removed, cut into bite-size pieces

Crusty bread, for serving (optional)

In a large heavy-bottomed pot, heat the olive oil over medium-high heat. Add the onion, carrots, and celery and sauté, stirring occasionally until the vegetables are soft and the onion is translucent, 3–4 minutes. Stir in the garlic and sauté, stirring occasionally, until fragrant, about 1 minute. Add the cumin, coriander, and red pepper flakes, if using, and sauté, stirring constantly, until fragrant, about 2 minutes. Season to taste with salt and pepper. Add the vegetable stock, the tomatoes and their juices, and the lentils, and bring to a boil, stirring occasionally. Reduce the heat to low and simmer until thickened, 20–25 minutes. Stir in the kale and simmer over low heat until wilted, 1–2 minutes. Taste, and season generously with salt and pepper.

Serve in shallow bowls with crusty bread.

Store the soup, in an airtight container in the refrigerator, for up to 3 days, or in the freezer for up to 3 months. When reheating leftovers, you may need to add a little water, because this soup gets thicker the longer it sits.

*You can buy these at Whole Foods, beside the regular lentils—or you can sprout your own.

TOMATO-CHICKPEA CURRY WITH KALE

⊙   DF / GF / V

Serves 4, with leftovers

This vegan dish, served over brown rice, is incredibly satisfying—even my meat-loving husband enjoys it! The leftovers keep for several days in the refrigerator, and make for a wonderful reheat-at-work lunch.

4 tablespoons extra-virgin olive oil

1/2 medium red onion, halved and thinly sliced

3 cloves garlic, minced, divided

1 (1-inch) piece fresh ginger, peeled and grated (about 1 tablespoon total)

1 teaspoon curry powder

1 teaspoon ground cumin

1/2 teaspoon ground cinnamon

1/2 teaspoon ground coriander

1/2 teaspoon turmeric

1 (15-ounce) can chickpeas, rinsed and drained

1 (14.5-ounce) can whole peeled tomatoes with their juices

1/2 teaspoon agave nectar

3 tablespoons chopped fresh cilantro leaves

Fine sea salt and freshly ground black pepper

2 bunches Tuscan (Lacinato) kale, stems removed, cut into bite-size pieces

Cooked brown rice, lemon wedges, and yogurt (optional), for serving

In a large heavy-bottomed pot, heat 2 tablespoons of the olive oil over medium-high heat. Add the onion and sauté, stirring occasionally, until translucent, 3–4 minutes. Add 2 cloves of the garlic and the ginger and sauté, stirring occasionally, until fragrant, about 1 minute. Add the curry powder, cumin, cinnamon, coriander, and turmeric, and sauté, stirring constantly, until fragrant, for 2 minutes. Add the chickpeas and stir well to incorporate.

In a medium bowl, use your hands to crush the tomatoes. Add the tomatoes and their juice to the sauté pan, along with the agave nectar, and let the mixture come to a boil. Reduce the heat to low and simmer, uncovered, until thickened, about 10 minutes. If the curry gets too dry, add a bit of water. Stir in the cilantro and season to taste with salt and pepper.

In a large skillet, heat the remaining 2 tablespoons olive oil over medium-high heat. Add the remaining 1 clove garlic and sauté, stirring occasionally, until fragrant, about 1 minute. Add the kale and sauté, stirring occasionally, for 2 minutes. Add 1/4 cup of water and steam the kale, stirring occasionally, until wilted, 2–3 minutes. Season to taste with salt and pepper.

Serve the curry in shallow bowls, along with brown rice and the sautéed kale. Garnish with a squeeze of lemon, and, if you're not vegan, a dollop of yogurt.

Store any leftovers, in an airtight container in the refrigerator, for up to 3 days, or in the freezer, for up to 3 months.

VARIATION: Dice one medium eggplant, toss with 1 tablespoon olive oil, and season to taste with salt and pepper. Spread on an aluminum foil-lined baking sheet and roast at 425°F until lightly browned, 20–25 minutes. Make the recipe as instructed above, but add the eggplant to the curry when you add the chickpeas and tomatoes. Stir in 3 tablespoons chopped mint at the end, along with the cilantro.

DF / GF

LAMB TAGINE WITH APRICOTS & FIGS

Serves 4, with leftovers | Serve with Citrus Salad with Arugula & Ricotta Salata (page 136)

I tasted lamb tagine for the first time many years ago in Paris, and fell completely in love with its exotic blend of sweet and savory spices, not to mention its beautiful colors and varied textures. This is a dish that's even better made in advance, so prepare it the day before and gently reheat it before serving.

2 tablespoons extra-virgin olive oil

1 1/2 pounds lamb shoulder (or lamb stew meat), cut into 1 1/2-inch chunks

Fine sea salt and freshly ground black pepper

1 medium white or yellow onion, chopped

1 large carrot, peeled and chopped

1 rib celery, chopped

2 teaspoons ground cumin

1 teaspoon ground cinnamon

1/2 teaspoon ground ginger

1/2 teaspoon ground nutmeg

1/2 teaspoon ground cloves

1/2 teaspoon ground allspice

1 (14.5-ounce) can diced tomatoes and their juices

2–3 cups chicken stock

1 (15-ounce) can chickpeas, rinsed and drained

1 cup dried apricots

1 cup (stemmed and halved) dried Black Mission figs

1/2 cup chopped fresh mint leaves, plus more for garnish

Couscous*, for serving

In a large Dutch oven, heat the olive oil over medium-high heat. Season the lamb with salt and pepper and add it to the Dutch oven. Cook the lamb, turning it often, until browned on all sides, about 5 minutes. Remove the lamb to a bowl and set aside. With the Dutch oven over medium-high heat, add the onion, carrot, and celery and sauté, stirring occasionally, until the vegetables are soft and the onion is translucent, 3–4 minutes. Add the cumin, cinnamon, ginger, nutmeg, cloves, and allspice and sauté, stirring constantly, until fragrant, about 2 minutes. Add the tomatoes and their juices and 2 cups of the chicken stock and bring to a boil. Reduce the heat to low, add the lamb back to the Dutch oven, and season to taste with salt. Cover and simmer the mixture, stirring occasionally, until thickened, about 1 hour.

Add the chickpeas, apricots, and figs, and continue simmering, stirring occasionally, until the meat is fork-tender, 1–1 1/2 hours. Add additional stock as needed—you want plenty of the fragrant sauce. Season to taste with additional salt and pepper as necessary. Stir in the chopped mint. Serve over couscous, garnished with additional chopped, fresh mint.

DO AHEAD: The tagine can be made ahead, and kept in an airtight container in the refrigerator for up to 3 days, or frozen for up to 3 months. Reheat gently in a Dutch oven over medium heat, adding water as needed, and garnish with fresh mint.

*Eliminate the couscous if you have a gluten-allergy.

QUPÉ SYRAH, CENTRAL COAST, 2011 ($$)

Enjoy this classically styled Syrah, from the Central Coast of California, with this flavorful tagine. A Pioneer of Syrah in the US, Qupé's 2011 has aromas of ripe berries, spices, and licorice, and is relatively low in alcohol. It's vibrancy and spice-box aromas work well with this dish.

USA
Biodynamic
$18.99

07 | SALADS & SIDES

SPRING

Salade de Chèvre Chaud (Warm Goat Cheese Salad) | 109

Spring Salad with Fava Beans, Peas & Radishes | 110

Spring Pea Risotto | 112

SUMMER

Heirloom Caprese Salad | 115

Greek Peasant Salad | 116

Mediterranean Quinoa Salad with Roasted Summer Vegetables | 119

Grilled Portobello Mushroom Salad with Mixed Greens & Roasted Peppers | 121

Roasted Vegetable Ratatouille | 122

Haricots Verts with Dijon Vinaigrette | 124

FALL

Detox Kale Salad | 127

Endive Salad with Pears, Blue Cheese & Walnuts | 129

Red Quinoa Salad with Butternut Squash & Spinach | 130

Arugula, Radicchio & Fennel Salad | 132

Farro with Wild Mushrooms | 135

WINTER

Citrus Salad with Arugula & Ricotta Salata | 136

Spinach Salad with Roasted Chicken & Oranges | 139

Roasted Winter Squash with Kale & Pomegranate Seeds | 140

Shaved Brussels Sprout & Endive Salad | 142

Broccoli Rabe with Pine Nuts & Golden Raisins | 144

Simple Roasted Broccoli (or Cauliflower) | 146

Roasted Fingerling Potatoes | 146

Whole-Roasted Carrots with Orange, Thyme & Garlic | 149

SALADE DE CHÈVRE CHAUD (WARM GOAT CHEESE SALAD)

Serves 4

This is my all-time favorite salad, and the first thing I order when I go to Paris. I like to add thinly sliced watermelon radish and Granny Smith apple, for a little extra color and crunch.

2 teaspoons whole grain Dijon mustard

2 tablespoons red wine vinegar

1/4 cup extra-virgin olive oil, plus more for drizzling

Fine sea salt and freshly ground black pepper

8 packed cups mixed lettuces, torn into bite-size pieces

4 small radishes, thinly sliced

1/2 watermelon radish, halved and thinly sliced into half-moons

1/2 Granny Smith apple, thinly sliced

8 (1/2-inch-thick) whole grain baguette slices

3 ounces aged goat cheese, cut into 8 slices

Preheat the broiler to high.

In a small bowl, whisk together the mustard and red wine vinegar. Add 1/4 cup olive oil in a slow, steady stream, whisking constantly. Season to taste with salt and pepper.

In a large bowl, toss together the lettuces, both types of radishes, and the apple.

Arrange the baguette slices on a baking sheet and drizzle with olive oil. Broil until beginning to brown, about 30 seconds. Remove from the oven, flip over, and top with the goat cheese slices. Broil until bubbling and browned, about 1 minute. (Stand right by the oven—these can quickly burn if you don't watch them!)

Drizzle the vinaigrette over the salad, and gently toss. Season with additional salt and pepper. Divide among four plates and top each with 2 warm goat cheese crostini. Serve immediately.

VARIATION: You can make more of a composed salad if you like, arranging the watermelon radishes on the bottom of the plate, drizzling with vinaigrette, and then adding the remaining salad (lettuces, radishes, and apple) and goat cheese toasts on top. Or you can serve it family style, by tossing all the salad ingredients in a big bowl, and serving the goat cheese toasts on the side.

DOMAINE PIERRE MOREY, BOURGOGNE-ALIGOTE, 2011 ($$)

A little known grape from Burgundy, and the traditional wine used in the preparation of a Kir, Aligote is vibrant and steely, and a perfect companion for goat cheese. This one is made by Pierre Morey, one of Burgundy's most respected winemakers.

France

Biodynamic

$17.99

SPRING SALAD WITH FAVA BEANS, PEAS & RADISHES

⊙ GF

Serves 4 | Serve with Roasted Salmon with Honey-Dijon Glaze (page 185)

Fava beans are, admittedly, a lot of work—they require shelling, blanching, and peeling. But they're one of my favorite vegetables, and given that they're only available a few months out of the year, it's completely worth the effort. Enlist a friend (or child or spouse) to help. And to save time, blanch the favas and peas a day in advance, then just toss the salad together before serving.

1 cup fresh shelled fava beans
(about 1 1/2 pounds in the pod)
1 cup fresh shelled peas (about 1 pound in the pod)
6 packed cups baby arugula
6 breakfast radishes, thinly sliced
1/4 cup chopped fresh mint leaves

2 tablespoons grated lemon zest, plus 2 tablespoons
freshly squeezed lemon juice (2 lemons)
1/4 cup extra-virgin olive oil
Fine sea salt and freshly ground black pepper
1/4 cup freshly grated Pecorino, plus more for garnish

Bring a medium pot of salted water to boil, and prepare a bowl of ice water.

Place the fava beans in the boiling water and cook until they're softened and you can see bright green through the white skin, 4–5 minutes. Use a slotted spoon to lift the fava beans from the boiling water and plunge them into the ice water; reserve the boiling water. Let the fava beans sit in the ice water until cool, then use the slotted spoon to transfer them to a large bowl; reserve the ice water. Slip the white skins off the fava beans and discard the skins.

Add some more ice to the water bath. Place the peas in the boiling water and cook until bright green, about 1 minute. Use a slotted spoon to lift the peas from the boiling water and plunge them into the ice water. Let the peas sit in the ice water until cool, then use the slotted spoon to transfer them to the bowl with the fava beans. Add the arugula, radishes, and mint.

Pour the lemon zest and juice into a small bowl. Add the olive oil in a slow, steady stream, whisking constantly. Season to taste with salt and pepper. Drizzle over the salad and toss gently to combine. Add the Pecorino and toss gently to combine. Taste and add more Pecorino, lemon juice, salt, or pepper if you like. Serve immediately.

DO AHEAD: The fava beans and peas can be blanched a day ahead, and stored in an airtight container in the refrigerator.

SPRING PEA RISOTTO

Serves 4 | Serve with Roasted Chicken with Lemon, Thyme & Shallots (page 179)

GF

I love making risotto. There's something really therapeutic about standing and stirring for nearly 20 minutes—preferably with a glass of wine in hand! Risotto is best served immediately, though you can make it in advance and reheat it on the stove, adding in extra stock to loosen it up a bit.

1 cup fresh shelled peas* (about 1 pound in the pod)

3 cups chicken or vegetable stock

2 tablespoons extra-virgin olive oil

1 small white or yellow onion, finely chopped

1 cup Arborio rice

1/2 cup dry white wine

2 tablespoons grated lemon zest, plus 3 tablespoons freshly squeezed lemon juice (2 lemons)

1/4 cup freshly grated Pecorino or Parmesan, plus more for serving

2 tablespoons unsalted butter

2 tablespoons chopped fresh flat-leaf parsley leaves or mint leaves

Fine sea salt and freshly ground black pepper

Bring a medium pot of salted water to a boil, and prepare a bowl of ice water. Add the peas to the boiling water and cook until bright green, about 1 minute. Drain the peas and quickly plunge them into the ice water. Let the peas sit in the ice water until cool, then drain again.

In a medium saucepan, bring the chicken or vegetable stock to a simmer. Keep warm on the stove while you make the risotto.

In a large heavy-bottomed sauté pan (or pot), heat the olive oil over medium heat. Add the onion and sauté until translucent, 3–4 minutes. Add the rice and cook, stirring with a wooden spoon, until the grains are coated with oil and have turned opaque, 2–3 minutes. Add the white wine and cook, stirring, until the liquid is almost completely absorbed, 1–2 minutes. Add 1/2 cup of the warm stock and cook, stirring frequently (but not constantly), until all of the stock is absorbed. Continue adding 1/2 cups of stock in this manner until all of the stock has been added and the rice is al dente, about 18 minutes total. The rice should look creamy and tender at this point. Stir in the peas, lemon zest and juice, 1/4 cup Pecorino or Parmesan, butter, and parsley or mint. Season to taste with salt and pepper. Remove from the heat, cover, and let sit for 2–3 minutes, then serve immediately. I like to bring a hunk of Pecorino or Parmesan to the table with a grater, so everyone can grate a little extra cheese over their risotto.

*If you can't find fresh peas, you can substitute 1 cup of frozen peas. No need to thaw, just follow the recipe as written, adding an additional minute to the boiling time for the peas.

GF ◉

HEIRLOOM CAPRESE SALAD

Serves 4

Tomato season is a highlight of the year for me, especially when I can find colorful heirloom varieties at the farmers' market. This salad is super easy to make, but using top-quality ingredients is key.

1 1/2 pounds heirloom tomatoes, in assorted colors and sizes, cut into 1/2-inch-thick slices

8 ounces fresh buffalo mozzarella, cut into 1/2-inch-thick slices

1/2 cup halved yellow and red grape or cherry tomatoes

1/2 cup torn fresh basil leaves

2 tablespoons balsamic vinegar

4 tablespoons extra-virgin olive oil

Fine sea salt and freshly ground black pepper

Crusty bread, for serving (optional)

Alternate the tomatoes and mozzarella slices on a platter and scatter the cherry tomatoes and basil on top.

Pour the balsamic vinegar into a small bowl. Add the olive oil in a slow, steady stream, whisking constantly. Season to taste with salt and pepper then drizzle over the salad. Serve with crusty bread to soak up the juices!

GREEK PEASANT SALAD

Serves 4

I like using a combination of red and yellow grape tomatoes in this summery salad. Marinate the red onion in red wine vinegar while you prep the other ingredients—it helps take the bite out.

1 small red onion, halved and thinly sliced into half-moons

2 tablespoons red wine vinegar

1 English cucumber, halved lengthwise, seeded, and cut into 1/2-inch chunks

1 pint grape or cherry tomatoes, halved

2 ounces Greek or French block feta, cut into cubes

1/4 cup pitted, halved Kalamata olives

1/4 cup chopped fresh mint leaves

1/4 cup extra-virgin olive oil

Fine sea salt and freshly ground black pepper

Warm pita bread, for serving*

In a large bowl, stir together the red onion and red wine vinegar. Let sit for 10 minutes. Add the cucumber, tomatoes, feta, olives, and mint, drizzle with olive oil, season to taste with salt and pepper, and toss gently to combine.

Serve immediately with warm pita bread to soak up the extra vinaigrette.

*Eliminate the pita if you have a gluten sensitivity.

DF / GF / V ◉

MEDITERRANEAN QUINOA SALAD WITH ROASTED SUMMER VEGETABLES

Serves 4

Make this colorful salad for a picnic or an outdoor dinner party. It tastes great at room temperature and you can prep the whole thing a full day in advance. In fact, the flavors are actually better the second day.

1/2 medium eggplant, diced

1 small zucchini, diced

1 small summer squash, diced

3 tablespoons extra-virgin olive oil, divided

Fine sea salt and freshly ground black pepper

2 tablespoons freshly squeezed lemon juice (1 lemon)

1 clove garlic, minced

1/2 cup halved grape tomatoes

1 cup cooked (white, red, or mixed) quinoa, cooled

2 tablespoons chopped fresh basil leaves

2 tablespoons chopped fresh mint leaves

2 tablespoons toasted pine nuts

Crumbled feta (optional)

Preheat the oven to 425°F. Line 2 baking sheets with aluminum foil.

Divide the eggplant, zucchini, and summer squash between the 2 foil-lined baking sheets, drizzle with 1 tablespoon of the olive oil, season to taste with salt and pepper, and toss to combine. Roast until softened and beginning to brown, about 30 minutes. Cool to room temperature.

In a large bowl, whisk together the lemon juice and garlic. Add the remaining 2 tablespoons of the olive oil in a slow, steady stream, whisking constantly. Season to taste with salt and pepper. Add the tomatoes, quinoa, basil, mint, and roasted vegetables, and gently stir to combine. Taste and adjust the seasoning as needed. Garnish with toasted pine nuts and feta, if using. Serve at room temperature.

Store, in an airtight container in the refrigerator, up to 3 days.

GF ◉

GRILLED PORTOBELLO MUSHROOM SALAD WITH MIXED GREENS & ROASTED PEPPERS

Serves 4 | Serve with Grilled Skirt Steak with Chimichurri (page 192)

In this hearty vegetarian salad, the marinade used for the grilled portobello mushrooms doubles as the vinaigrette. To save time, roast the peppers a day in advance. Though I love goat cheese in this dish, feel free to swap it out for blue cheese, shaved Parmesan, or Manchego.

4 portobello mushrooms, stems removed and gills scraped

4 sprigs fresh thyme

1/4 cup balsamic vinegar

4 cloves garlic, minced

1/2 cup extra-virgin olive oil

1 red bell pepper

1 yellow bell pepper

1 tablespoon canola oil

Fine sea salt and freshly ground black pepper

6 packed cups mixed baby greens

1/2 red onion, halved and thinly sliced into half-moons

1/2 cup crumbled goat cheese (about 2 ounces)

1/4 cup toasted pine nuts (optional)

Place the mushrooms and thyme in a large re-sealable plastic bag (or in a large bowl).

In a small bowl, whisk together the balsamic vinegar and garlic. Add the olive oil in slow, steady stream, whisking constantly. Pour over the mushrooms and seal the bag (or cover the bowl with plastic wrap). Marinate, at room temperature, for 1 hour. (You can marinate for 30 minutes if you're in a hurry.)

While the mushrooms marinate, roast the peppers: If you have gas burners, place each pepper on a separate burner and turn the flames to high. Roast, turning every 2 minutes with tongs, until completely charred on the outside, 8–9 minutes. (If you don't have gas burners, place the peppers on a foil-lined baking sheet and broil on high, turning as necessary, until they are completely charred on the outside, about 15 minutes.) Place the peppers in a large heatproof bowl, cover with plastic wrap, and let steam for 15 minutes.

When the peppers are cool enough to handle, remove the burnt skins. Cut the peppers in half and remove the seeds. (You can hold the peppers under running water to help remove the skin and seeds, but it will take away some of the flavor!) Cut the peppers into thin strips.

Heat a grill pan over high heat and brush with 1 tablespoon canola oil. Remove the mushrooms from the bag and season on both sides with salt and pepper. Pour the remaining marinade into a large bowl; discard the thyme. Grill the mushrooms, flipping once, until softened, 3–4 minutes per side. (NOTE: If you're using an outdoor grill, set the heat at medium and follow the same instructions.) Transfer to a cutting board, let cool slightly, then cut into strips. Add the mushroom strips and the roasted peppers to the bowl with the reserved marinade, and let sit for 10 minutes. Add the mixed greens and red onion, and toss to combine. Season to taste with salt and pepper. Top the salad with goat cheese and pine nuts.

VARIATION: This is really delicious with grilled chicken or steak. Just make some extra balsamic marinade to marinate the meat as well (in a separate bag)!

BLOOMER CREEK, "VIN D'ETE" CABERNET FRANC, FINGER LAKES, 2011 ($$$)

USA

Organic

$21.99

Fragrant, peppery, with light bell pepper notes, this supple Cabernet Franc from New York State's Finger Lakes region perfectly echoes the earthiness of this salad.

ROASTED VEGETABLE RATATOUILLE

DF / GF / V

Serves 4

This is my ode to Provence, where I first fell in love with the classic vegetable- and tomato-laden side dish. Unlike most ratatouille recipes, for mine, I like to roast the vegetables first to intensify their flavors, before simmering them on the stovetop. This is delicious with grilled chicken or salmon, or as a vegetarian dish served over couscous or quinoa.

1/4 cup, plus 2 tablespoons extra-virgin olive oil

1 small eggplant, cut into 1/2-inch pieces

1 small zucchini, cut into 1/2-inch pieces

1 small yellow squash, cut into 1/2-inch pieces

Fine sea salt and freshly ground black pepper

1 pint grape tomatoes, halved if large

1 small red onion, diced

1 small red or yellow bell pepper, cored, seeded, and diced

2 cloves garlic, minced

1 (28-ounce) can whole peeled tomatoes with their juices

1 tablespoon balsamic vinegar

1/2 cup chopped fresh basil leaves

Shaved Parmesan, for serving (optional)

Preheat the oven to 425°F. Line two baking sheets with aluminum foil.

In a large bowl, toss the eggplant, zucchini, and squash with 3 tablespoons of the olive oil. Season to taste with salt and pepper. Spread the mixture onto 1 1/2 of the foil-lined baking sheets. Add the grape tomatoes to the large bowl and toss with 1 tablespoon of the olive oil. Season to taste with salt and pepper. Spread out onto the empty half of the 1 baking sheet. Roast until the vegetables are softened and beginning to brown, about 30 minutes. Transfer to a rack and let cool slightly.

While the vegetables are roasting, make the tomato sauce: In a large heavy-bottomed pot, heat the remaining 2 tablespoons olive oil over medium-high heat. Add the red onion and red bell pepper and sauté, stirring occasionally, until the onion is translucent and the pepper is softened, 3–4 minutes. Add the garlic and sauté, stirring occasionally, until fragrant, about 1 minute. Add the canned tomatoes, smashing them gently with a spoon, and simmer, uncovered, for 10 minutes. Add the roasted vegetables, stir, and simmer for 5 minutes. Stir in the balsamic vinegar and basil and season to taste with salt and pepper.

Serve in bowls with shaved Parmesan (if desired).

DO AHEAD: This dish tastes even better on the second or third day, so make it a few days in advance and just reheat on the stovetop before serving. Store, in an airtight container in the refrigerator for up to 5 days, or freeze for up to 3 months.

HARICOTS VERTS WITH DIJON VINAIGRETTE

DF / GF / V

Serves 4

I love serving this light, French-inspired side dish as part of a decadent holiday buffet. It's also perfect in the summertime, as it's intended to be served at room temperature or chilled.

1 pound haricots verts, ends trimmed

1 tablespoon red wine vinegar

2 teaspoons whole grain Dijon mustard

1 shallot, minced

3 tablespoons extra-virgin olive oil

Fine sea salt and freshly ground black pepper

Bring a large pot of salted water to a boil, and prepare a bowl of ice water. Add the haricots verts to the boiling water and cook until bright green and still slightly crisp, 3–4 minutes. Drain the beans and quickly plunge them into the ice water. Let the green beans sit until cool, then drain again. Pat dry the green beans and place in a large bowl.

In a small bowl, whisk together the vinegar, mustard, and shallot. Add the olive oil in a slow, steady stream, whisking constantly. Season to taste with salt and pepper.

Drizzle the vinaigrette over the beans and toss to coat evenly. Season to taste with salt and pepper. Place on a platter and serve immediately.

DO AHEAD: Blanch the beans a day ahead, wrap in paper towels, and store, in a resealable plastic bag in the refrigerator, for up to 1 day. Make the vinaigrette and toss with the beans just before serving.

DF / GF / V ◉

DETOX KALE SALAD

Serves 4, with leftovers | Serve with Spicy Black Bean Soup (page 92)

This is my go-to lunch. I call it a detox salad, because it's packed with nutrient-rich vegetables and has protein from the quinoa. To save time, I stop by the Whole Foods salad bar and stock up on shredded carrots, red cabbage, and cooked quinoa. Feel free to toss in some roast chicken if you want a heartier meal.

*4 packed cups chopped kale (curly, Lacinato, red,
    or a combination), stems removed*
1 cup shredded carrots (from about 2 medium carrots)
1 cup shredded red cabbage (from about 1/8 head cabbage)
3/4 cup cooked quinoa, cooled

1 avocado, peeled, pitted, and cubed
2 tablespoons freshly squeezed lemon juice (1 lemon)
1/4 cup extra-virgin olive oil
Fine sea salt and freshly ground black pepper

In a large bowl, toss together the kale, carrots, cabbage, quinoa, and avocado.

Pour the lemon juice into a small bowl. Add the olive oil in a slow, steady stream, whisking constantly. Season to taste with salt and pepper. Drizzle over the salad and toss to combine. Taste and add additional salt and pepper, or another splash of lemon if you like. Serve immediately.

Store the salad, in an airtight container in the refrigerator, up to 1 day.

GF ◉

ENDIVE SALAD WITH PEARS, BLUE CHEESE & WALNUTS

Serves 4 | Serve with Butternut Squash Soup with Spiced Pears (page 94)

This pretty combination of endive, pear, and blue cheese embodies fall to me. Red Belgian endive can be hard to find, but Trader Joe's always seems to have it.

1 shallot, minced

1 tablespoon sherry vinegar

1 teaspoon honey

3 tablespoons extra-virgin olive oil

Fine sea salt and freshly ground black pepper

3 small red Belgian endives

3 small yellow Belgian endives

1 pear

1 lemon wedge

2 ounces blue cheese, crumbled

1/4 cup coarsely chopped, toasted walnuts

In a small bowl, whisk together the shallot, vinegar, and honey. Add the olive oil in a slow, steady stream, whisking constantly. Season to taste with salt and pepper.

Cut the tough bottoms off of each endive and separate the leaves.

Thinly slice the pear and squeeze the lemon wedge over the slices to keep them from browning.

Divide the endive leaves and pear slices among four plates. Sprinkle with blue cheese and toasted walnuts, and drizzle with the vinaigrette. Serve immediately.

RED QUINOA SALAD WITH BUTTERNUT SQUASH & SPINACH

DF / GF / V

Serves 4

This salad was inspired by a similar dish my friend Dori made for me several years ago. I loved it so much that I recreated it that very same week, adding in some leftover quinoa and toasted pine nuts. A new favorite was born.

2 cups peeled, cubed butternut squash

1 small red onion, halved and sliced into half-moons

3 tablespoons extra-virgin olive oil, divided

1/4 teaspoon cayenne

Fine sea salt and freshly ground black pepper

4 packed cups baby spinach

1/2 cup dried cranberries

1 cup cooked red quinoa, cooled

2 teaspoons balsamic vinegar

1/4 cup toasted pine nuts

Preheat the oven to 425°F. Line a baking sheet with aluminum foil.

Arrange the butternut squash and onion on the foil-lined baking sheet, drizzle with 1 tablespoon of the olive oil, sprinkle with cayenne, season to taste with salt and pepper, and toss to combine. Roast, stirring occasionally, until tender and just beginning to brown, about 30 minutes.

While the squash is roasting, steam the spinach: Fill a medium saucepan with 2 inches of water, set a steamer basket, on top, and bring the water to a boil. Lower the heat so that the water is simmering then add the spinach to the steamer basket and steam until bright green and slightly wilted, about 2 minutes. Drain in a colander and squeeze out any excess water.

In a large bowl, stir together the squash, onion, spinach, cranberries, and quinoa.

Pour the balsamic vinegar into a small bowl. Add the remaining 2 tablespoons of the olive oil in a slow, steady stream, whisking constantly. Season to taste with salt and pepper. Drizzle over the quinoa mixture and toss to combine. Season to taste with salt and pepper. Serve warm or at room temperature.

Store, in an airtight container in the refrigerator, for up to 3 days.

ARUGULA, RADICCHIO & FENNEL SALAD

⊙ DF / GF / V

Serves 4–6 | Serve with Spicy Seafood Stew (page 97)

This is such a light, refreshing salad, and the perfect accompaniment to a heavier main dish like pasta or roasted meat. A mandoline is helpful to cut paper-thin slices of fennel, but if you don't have one, a sharp knife will work.

4 packed cups baby arugula

1 small head radicchio halved, cored, and very thinly sliced

1 small fennel bulb, cored and very thinly sliced

2 tablespoons freshly squeezed lemon juice, or more to taste (1 lemon)

1/4 cup extra-virgin olive oil

Fine sea salt and freshly ground black pepper

1/2 cup freshly shaved Parmesan*

1/4 cup toasted walnuts (optional)

In a large bowl, toss together the arugula, radicchio, and fennel.

Pour the lemon juice into a small bowl. Add the olive oil in a slow, steady stream, whisking constantly. Season to taste with salt and pepper. Taste the vinaigrette—feel free to add more lemon juice if you want a more tart vinaigrette. Drizzle over the salad and toss to combine. Sprinkle with Parmesan and toasted walnuts, if using.

VARIATION: This salad is delicious with sliced oranges and toasted hazelnuts (in lieu of the walnuts), or ricotta salata in lieu of Parmesan.

*Eliminate the cheese to make this a dairy-free, vegan salad.

DF / V ⊙

FARRO WITH WILD MUSHROOMS

Serves 4

Every Thanksgiving and Christmas, my mom makes a deliciously buttery, mushroom-studded brown rice. This is my healthier take, made with nutty farro and a blend of wild mushrooms.

1 1/4 cups semi-pearled farro

1 1/2 tablespoons extra-virgin olive oil, plus more
    for drizzling

2 cloves garlic, minced

1/2 shallot, minced

3/4 pound assorted mushrooms (cremini, shiitake,
    chanterelle, porcini, etc.), cleaned, trimmed, and sliced

1/2 tablespoon fresh thyme leaves, plus more for garnish

Fine sea salt and freshly ground black pepper

2 tablespoons dry white wine

Place the farro in a large heavy-bottomed pot and cover with cold water. Let soak for 15–20 minutes while you prep your other ingredients. Drain the farro and return it to the pot. Cover the farro with 2 quarts (8 cups) of water and bring to a boil. Reduce the heat to low and simmer, uncovered, until the grains are tender but still slightly chewy, about 25 minutes; drain and return to the pot.

While the farro is cooking, in a large skillet, heat 1 1/2 tablespoons of the olive oil over medium-high heat. Add the garlic and shallot and sauté, stirring occasionally, until fragrant, about 2 minutes. Add the mushrooms and thyme and sauté, stirring occasionally, until the mushrooms are softened, 5–7 minutes. Season generously with salt and pepper. Add the wine and simmer until evaporated, 2–3 minutes. Remove from the heat.

Using a wooden spoon, scrape the mushroom mixture into the pot with the cooked farro, and stir to combine. Season to taste with salt and pepper, and let cool slightly before serving.

Serve in a large bowl and garnish with additional thyme, and drizzle with olive oil.

DO AHEAD: Cook the farro-mushroom mixture 1–2 days in advance and keep, covered, in the refrigerator. Just before serving, heat 1 tablespoon olive oil in a skillet over medium heat. Add the farro-mushroom mixture and sauté, stirring frequently, until heated through, 2–3 minutes. Season with additional salt and pepper (if needed) and garnish with additional thyme.

DOMAINE DES BILLARDS, SAINT-AMOUR, 2011 ($$)

I like the contrast between the upfront red fruit and minerality of this Gamay from Southern Burgundy, and the earthy flavor of the farro and mushrooms. Saint-Amour, whose name means "Saint-Love," is one of the greatest villages of the Beaujolais region.

France
Organic
$19.99

CITRUS SALAD WITH ARUGULA & RICOTTA SALATA

⊙ GF

Serves 4–6

This has to be one of the prettiest salads I've ever seen. It was inspired by my brother-in-law Peter, who made it for us right after proposing to my sister...smart man! While it's best made in the winter, during blood orange and Cara Cara orange season, the rest of the year, feel free to use navel oranges.

1/2 small red onion, halved and thinly sliced into half-moons

1/4 cup white balsamic vinegar, divided

2 blood oranges

1 Cara Cara orange

1 navel orange

3 packed cups baby arugula

2 tablespoons extra-virgin olive oil

Fine sea salt and freshly ground black pepper

2 tablespoons roughly chopped fresh mint leaves

2 tablespoons roughly chopped, roasted, salted pistachios

2 tablespoons crumbled ricotta salata

Place the onion and 3 tablespoons of the white balsamic vinegar in a small bowl and let sit for at least 15 minutes and up to 3 hours. Drain the onions and set them aside; discard the vinegar.

Using a sharp knife, cut the ends off each orange, so they can sit flat on a cutting board. With smooth, downward strokes, cut the skin off 1 orange in sections—you want to remove the white pith and see the orange flesh beneath. Repeat with the remaining oranges. Turn each orange on its side and cut crosswise into thin round slices.

Place the arugula in a medium bowl. Pour the remaining 1 tablespoon vinegar into a small bowl. Add the olive oil in a slow, steady stream, whisking constantly. Drizzle over the arugula, season to taste with salt and pepper, and toss to combine.

Arrange the orange slices in alternating colors on a large plate or platter. Sprinkle with mint, pistachios, and the marinated red onions. Pile the arugula in the center of the oranges and sprinkle with ricotta salata. Serve immediately.

DF / GF

SPINACH SALAD WITH ROASTED CHICKEN & ORANGES

Serves 4–6

I created this super-easy salad one day while cleaning out the fridge, tossing together whatever odds and ends I had. As it turns out, it was actually really good! Sliced avocado or crumbled feta would make nice additions.

2 oranges (I especially love Cara Cara)

6 packed cups baby spinach

3/4 cup cooked quinoa, cooled

1/2 cup canned chickpeas, rinsed and drained

1 small red onion, halved and thinly sliced into half-moons

2 roasted or grilled chicken breasts, thinly sliced

2 tablespoons white balsamic vinegar

1/4 cup extra-virgin olive oil

Fine sea salt and freshly ground black pepper

Crumbled feta (optional)

Using a sharp knife, cut the ends off each orange so they can sit flat on a cutting board. With smooth, downward strokes, cut the skin off 1 orange in sections—you want to remove the white pith and see the orange flesh beneath. Once the skin is removed, hold 1 orange over a large bowl. Use a small sharp knife to carefully cut in between the membranes to remove the sections of the orange. Let each section, along with its juices, drop into the bowl. Repeat with the remaining orange. Discard the peels and membranes. Add the spinach, quinoa, chickpeas, red onions, and chicken and toss gently to combine.

Pour the white balsamic vinegar into a small bowl. Add the olive oil in a slow, steady stream, whisking constantly. Season to taste with salt and pepper, drizzle over the salad, and toss to combine. Taste the salad and season with additional salt and pepper if you like. Garnish with crumbled feta, if using.

ROASTED WINTER SQUASH WITH KALE & POMEGRANATE SEEDS

◉ DF / GF / V

Serves 4

With its combination of dark green, red, and bright orange, this salad looks so festive. Though you can use any winter squash for this recipe, Delicata is both beautiful and practical—and unlike with other varieties, you can actually eat the skin.

1 pound winter squash, such as acorn, butternut, delicata, or kabocha

5 tablespoons extra-virgin olive oil, divided

Fine sea salt and freshly ground black pepper

2 tablespoons balsamic vinegar

1 bunch Tuscan (Lacinato) kale, stems removed, cut into bite-size pieces

2 tablespoons pomegranate seeds

2 tablespoons toasted pine nuts

Shaved Parmesan,* for garnish

Preheat the oven to 425°F. Line a baking sheet with aluminum foil.

Use a sharp knife to cut the squash in half then scoop out the seeds with a spoon. If using acorn or butternut squash, place the 2 halves, cut-side up, on the foil-lined baking sheet. If using delicata or kabocha squash, cut it into half-moons and arrange those on the foil-lined baking sheet. Brush the squash with 1 tablespoon of the olive oil, sprinkle with salt and pepper, and roast until soft (turn the delicata or kabocha squash once during roasting), 20 – 25 minutes for the delicata or kabocha squash and about 40 minutes for the acorn or butternut squash. Cool slightly. When cool enough to handle, cut the acorn or butternut squash into half-moon pieces.

Pour the balsamic vinegar into a small bowl. Add the remaining 4 tablespoons olive oil in a slow, steady stream, whisking constantly. Season to taste with salt and pepper.

Place the kale in a large bowl, add half the vinaigrette, and toss until evenly coated.

To assemble the salad, arrange the squash slices on a large platter—you can leave the skin on and people can cut it off themselves—and drizzle with the remaining vinaigrette. Arrange the kale on top then sprinkle with pomegranate seeds, pine nuts, and shaved Parmesan

DO AHEAD: The squash can be roasted ahead and kept at room temperature for several hours before using. Alternatively you can roast the squash 1 day ahead and keep it in an airtight container in the refrigerator for up to 1 day. Bring it to room temperature before using.

*Eliminate the Parmesan for a dairy-free, vegan salad.

⊙ GF

SHAVED BRUSSELS SPROUT & ENDIVE SALAD

Serves 6–8 | Serve with Parmesan Polenta with Sausage Ragù (page 215)

Discovering that I could eat raw Brussels sprouts was a revelation, and I've never turned back. This lemony salad makes a wonderful, light accompaniment to a heavier stew or pasta dish. It also pairs well with roasted chicken or fish.

1 1/2 pounds Brussels sprouts, very thinly sliced

1/2 pound yellow Belgian endives, very thinly sliced

1/2 pound red Belgian endives, very thinly sliced

2 tablespoons freshly-squeezed lemon juice,
*   plus more to taste (1 lemon)*

1/4 cup extra-virgin olive oil

Fine sea salt and freshly ground black pepper

1/2 cup freshly grated Pecorino

In a large bowl, toss together the Brussels sprouts and the red and yellow Belgian endive.

Pour the lemon juice into a small bowl. Add the olive oil in a slow, steady stream, whisking constantly. Season to taste with salt and pepper. Drizzle over the salad and toss to combine. Add the Pecorino and toss again. Taste the salad and season with additional salt, pepper, and lemon juice as needed. Let sit for 15 minutes to allow the flavors to blend; toss before serving.

DO AHEAD: Shave the Brussels sprouts and cut the endive several hours in advance, and keep them in a bowl in the refrigerator with moist paper towels on top. Before serving, toss with the vinaigrette and Pecorino, season with salt and pepper, and let sit for 15 minutes to allow the flavors to combine.

BROCCOLI RABE WITH PINE NUTS & GOLDEN RAISINS

DF / GF / V

Serves 4

Broccoli rabe's bitter taste takes some getting used to, but in this dish, I love how the golden raisins, red pepper flakes, and toasted pine nuts help balance it out. This makes an excellent side dish for grilled salmon, pork tenderloin, or meatballs with tomato sauce.

1 (1-pound) bunch broccoli rabe, tough ends removed, cut into 2-inch pieces

2 tablespoons extra-virgin olive oil

2 cloves garlic, thinly sliced

1/4 teaspoon red pepper flakes

3 tablespoons toasted pine nuts

3 tablespoons golden raisins

1 teaspoon balsamic vinegar

Fine sea salt and freshly ground black pepper

Bring a large pot of salted water to a boil, and prepare a bowl of ice water.

Add the broccoli rabe to the boiling water and boil until bright green, about 2 minutes. Using tongs, remove the broccoli rabe from the pot and place it in the ice water. Let the broccoli rabe sit in the ice water until cool, then drain it in a colander.

In a large skillet, heat the olive oil over medium-high heat. Add the garlic and red pepper flakes and sauté, stirring occasionally, until fragrant, about 1 minute. Add the broccoli rabe and sauté, stirring occasionally, until crisp-tender, 5–6 minutes. Transfer to a large bowl or platter then add the pine nuts, raisins, and balsamic vinegar and toss to combine. Season to taste with salt and pepper.

SIMPLE ROASTED BROCCOLI (OR CAULIFLOWER)

DF / GF / V

Serves 4

If you've never tried roasted broccoli or cauliflower, it will completely change your world. The salty, crispy combo is as addictive as French fries—only far healthier. Add grated Parmesan and a spritz of lemon for the ultimate side dish.

2 heads broccoli or 1 head cauliflower, stalks removed
2 tablespoons extra-virgin olive oil
Fine sea salt and freshly ground black pepper
Lemon wedges and freshly grated Parmesan, for serving (optional)

Preheat the oven to 425°F. Line a baking sheet with aluminum foil.

Break the broccoli or cauliflower into bite-size florets and place them on the foil-lined baking sheet. Drizzle with the olive oil, season to taste with salt and pepper, and roast until golden brown and beginning to turn dark on the edges, 25–30 minutes. Cool slightly before serving. If you like, toss with lemon juice and grated Parmesan.

ROASTED FINGERLING POTATOES

DF / GF / V

Serves 4

These crisp potatoes are the perfect companion to roast chicken or fish—or seared steak—and they couldn't be easier. Pop them in the oven while the rest of your dinner is cooking.

1 1/2 pounds fingerling (or baby) potatoes, halved lengthwise
2 tablespoons extra-virgin olive oil
Fine sea salt
8 thyme sprigs

Preheat the oven to 450°F. Line a baking sheet with aluminum foil.

Spread the potatoes out on the foil-lined baking sheet, drizzle with the olive oil, season to taste with salt, and toss to combine. Scatter with thyme sprigs and roast until golden brown and slightly crisp on the outside, 25–30 minutes.

DF / GF / V ◉

WHOLE-ROASTED CARROTS WITH ORANGE, THYME & GARLIC

Serves 4

I grew up hating cooked carrots—it wasn't until I tried them roasted that I came to love them. This recipe, inspired by one from Jamie Oliver, has you roast whole carrots with a medley of oranges, thyme, and garlic. If you can find multi-colored heirloom carrots, this dish is truly a show-stopper.

1 (1-pound) bunch (preferably multi-colored) carrots, rinsed and scrubbed, with the greens trimmed

1 tablespoons extra-virgin olive oil

1/2 orange, cut into wedges

2 cloves garlic, crushed and peeled

6 sprigs fresh thyme

Fine sea salt and freshly ground black pepper

Preheat the oven to 450°F. Line a baking sheet with aluminum foil.

Arrange the carrots on the foil-lined baking sheet and drizzle with the olive oil. Squeeze the juice from the orange wedges over the carrots then scatter the peels on top. Add the garlic cloves and thyme sprigs, season to taste with salt and pepper, and gently toss everything together. Cover the pan with foil and roast until the carrots are tender, about 25 minutes. Remove the foil and continue roasting until the carrots begin to brown, about 10 minutes. Season to taste with salt and pepper. Serve warm or at room temperature.

08 | SANDWICHES & SUCH

AVOCADO & RICOTTA TOASTS

Serves 2–4

I have a major thing for toast, and not just for breakfast. In fact, I regularly eat toast for lunch or dinner, usually with avocado or ricotta and some combination of the toppings below. Don't feel like you need to follow this recipe exactly, or to serve both types of toast in one meal—these are just suggestions. Most importantly, be sure to use a good-quality grainy bread.

RICOTTA TOPPING:

1/4 cup halved grape tomatoes

*1/2 tablespoon extra-virgin olive oil,
      plus more for drizzling*

Fine sea salt and freshly ground black pepper

1/2 cup fresh ricotta

1 tablespoon thinly sliced fresh basil

Thinly sliced prosciutto and arugula (optional)

AVOCADO TOPPING:

1 ripe avocado

*1 tablespoon freshly squeezed lemon juice, or more to
      taste (1 lemon)*

1/8 teaspoon red pepper flakes, or more to taste

Fine sea salt

Extra-virgin olive oil

Smoked salmon and thinly sliced lemon (optional)

TOAST:

4 (1/2-inch-thick) slices whole grain bread

FOR THE RICOTTA TOPPING:

Preheat the oven to 425°F. Line a baking sheet with aluminum foil.

Spread the tomatoes on the foil-lined baking sheet, drizzle with the 1/2 tablespoon olive oil, season to taste with salt and pepper, and toss to combine. Roast until softened, 15–20 minutes. Let cool slightly.

FOR THE AVOCADO TOPPING:

Cut the avocado in half, remove the pit, and scoop the flesh into a small bowl. Add the lemon juice and red pepper flakes, and use a fork to mash everything together. Season to taste with sea salt.

FOR THE TOAST:

Toast the bread.

To assemble, top 2 slices of toast with ricotta, a sprinkle of sea salt, and a drizzle of olive oil. Arrange the tomatoes on top and garnish with basil. Top each with a slice of prosciutto and a few arugula leaves, if using.

Top the remaining 2 slices of toast with the avocado mixture and drizzle with olive oil. Top each with smoked salmon and thinly sliced lemon, if desired.

SPROUTED WRAPS WITH LEMONY HUMMUS

Serves 4

Sprouted grains—essentially whole grains that have been allowed to germinate—are lower in starch, and higher in protein, vitamins, and minerals than traditional whole grain items. And they're more easily digestible for people with gluten sensitivities. You can find sprouted wraps in the frozen section of the grocery story near the gluten-free breads.

4 (8-inch) sprouted grain tortillas

1 cup Lemony Hummus (recipe follows)

3/4 cup grated carrots (about 2 medium carrots)

3/4 cup shredded red cabbage

2 packed cups mixed baby greens

3/4 cup crumbled feta

2 tablespoon freshly squeezed lemon juice (1 lemon)

Extra-virgin olive oil, for drizzling

Fine sea salt and freshly ground black pepper

In a non-stick skillet, warm the wraps over medium heat until pliable, 10–15 seconds. Spread each wrap with 1/4 cup hummus, leaving a 1-inch border. Layer the center of each wrap with carrots, cabbage, greens, and feta. Drizzle with lemon juice and olive oil and season to taste with salt and pepper. Roll each wrap up burrito-style and cut in half before serving.

VARIATION: If you don't want a vegetarian wrap, feel free to add some roast chicken or turkey. This is also delicious with roasted red peppers or chopped Kalamata olives.

DF / GF / V

LEMONY HUMMUS

Makes nearly 2 cups

It's amazing how often people buy hummus rather than making their own. Homemade tastes so much better, and it's also a lot better for you, as the store-bought versions are packed with preservatives. I love mine with lots of lemon, but feel free to cut back if it's not to your liking.

1 clove garlic, minced

1/2 teaspoon fine sea salt

1 (15-ounce) can chickpeas, rinsed and drained

1/4 cup extra-virgin olive oil, plus more to taste

*3 tablespoons freshly squeezed lemon juice,
     plus more to taste (1-2 lemons)*

2 tablespoons tahini

1 1/2 teaspoons ground cumin

1/8 teaspoon cayenne, plus more for serving

Place the garlic and 1/2 teaspoon salt on a cutting board and use the back of a fork to mash them into a paste. Transfer to a food processor and add the chickpeas, olive oil, lemon juice, tahini, cumin, and cayenne and process until smooth. Add a few tablespoons water if you like a thinner hummus. Taste the hummus and adjust the seasoning to your taste—you may like more salt, more lemon, more cumin, etc. (Keep in mind that once it sits for a few hours, the flavors will improve.) Serve with a drizzle of olive oil and a sprinkling of cayenne, and plenty of warm pita bread and/or raw vegetable slices.

Store, in an airtight container in the refrigerator, for up to 1 week.

DF

BAGUETTE SANDWICHES WITH DIJON CHICKEN SALAD

Makes 4 sandwiches

I love chicken salad (you pretty much have to if you grew up in Nashville!) but I'm not wild about all the mayonnaise. My version uses grainy Dijon mustard instead, plus green onions, and tarragon. All piled onto a baguette, this pretty much screams picnic.

1/4 cup freshly squeezed lemon juice (2 lemons)

2 tablespoons whole grain Dijon mustard

1/2 cup extra-virgin olive oil

Fine sea salt and freshly ground black pepper

2 cups shredded roast or rotisserie chicken (preferably white meat)

1/4 cup coarsely chopped, toasted pecans

1/4 cup thinly sliced green onions (white and light green parts only)

3 tablespoons chopped fresh tarragon leaves

2 whole grain or regular baguettes

Lettuce and thinly sliced cucumbers and radishes, for serving

In a large bowl, whisk together the lemon juice and mustard. Add the olive oil in a slow, steady stream, whisking constantly. Season generously with salt and pepper. Add the roast chicken, pecans, green onions, and tarragon and stir to combine.

Cut the ends off the 2 baguettes then cut them crosswise into 6-inch-long pieces and cut each piece in half horizontally. You'll have some pieces left over—save them for breakfast toast.

Divide the chicken salad mixture evenly amongst the 4 baguette bottoms, add some lettuce, along with cucumber and radishes, and place the remaining baguette halves on top.

Wrap each sandwich in parchment paper and tie with butchers' twine if you like. These are fine to transport to a picnic, but if you're going to be carrying them around for longer than an hour, bring a cooler with ice packs.

France

Organic

$14.99

JEAN-PAUL BRUN, DOMAINE DES TERRES DORRÉES, "L'ANCIEN" BEAUJOLAIS, 2013 ($$)

Forget Beaujolais Nouveau—this is the real thing. A freshly scented garden of sweet strawberries, but with enough kick to start a block party. Tasty and fruity, this wine begs to be opened in a meadow or by the river.

PANINI WITH ROSEMARY HAM, CHEDDAR & PEARS

Serves 4 | Serve with Arugula, Radicchio & Fennel Salad (page 132)

Feel free to use any type of ham and cheddar in this sandwich, or swap the sandwich rounds for loaf-style grainy bread. I love the combination of spicy mustard and pears; this sandwich is a fall weekend lunch favorite at our house.

*2 tablespoons whole grain Dijon mustard,
    plus more for serving*

4 thin, whole grain sandwich rounds,* split

4 slices rosemary ham

4 ounces thinly sliced (sharp or mild) white cheddar

1 ripe pear, thinly sliced

Extra-virgin olive oil, for brushing

Preheat a panini press, non-stick griddle, or large cast-iron skillet. (For anything on the stovetop, preheat the pan over medium-high heat.)

Spread Dijon mustard on each sandwich half. Divide the ham, cheddar, and pear slices among 4 sandwich bottoms then place the remaining sandwich halves on top. Brush the tops and bottoms of the sandwiches with olive oil.

Working in batches, press the sandwiches in the panini press until the bread is golden and the cheese begins to melt, 3–4 minutes total.

If you use a non-stick griddle or cast-iron skillet, place another pan on top of the sandwiches while they're cooking, to give them a nice crispy exterior, and be sure to flip them over midway through cooking.

Cut each sandwich in half and serve with extra Dijon mustard if you like.

*Ozery Bakery, a brand found at Whole Foods in the bakery section, makes thin sandwich rounds that are perfect for this recipe. Trader Joe's sells their own version as well. If you can't find the sandwich rounds, just use thinly-sliced whole grain sandwich bread.

Italy
Biodynamic
$19.99

RONCHI DI CIALLA, RIBOLLA GIALLA, COLLI ORIENTALI DEL FRIULI, 2012 ($$)

With its mix of herbal, salty, and sweet flavors, this panini demands a wine with range and some swagger. Ronchi di Cialla has single-handedly revived their small corner of Friuli since the early seventies, and their Ribolla—with it's high-toned, somewhat milky flavors—always gets me. Paired with rosemary, cheddar, and pears? Yes.

HEIRLOOM TOMATO PANINI WITH PROSCIUTTO & MOZZARELLA

Serves 4

You kind of can't go wrong with any combination of tomatoes, mozzarella, prosciutto, and basil—especially when it's in panini form. Feel free to use a large cast iron skillet or non-stick griddle.

1 large loaf fresh ciabatta bread

2 tablespoons extra-virgin olive oil, divided

8 ounces fresh buffalo or cow's milk mozzarella, thinly sliced

2 medium heirloom tomatoes, thinly sliced

4 thin slices prosciutto

1/3 cup torn fresh basil leaves

Fine sea salt and freshly ground black pepper

Preheat a panini press, non-stick griddle, or large cast-iron skillet. (For anything on the stovetop, preheat the pan over medium-high heat.)

Slice the ciabatta bread in half horizontally and drizzle both sides with about 1 tablespoon olive oil. Layer the bottom half with mozzarella, tomatoes, prosciutto, and torn basil. Season to taste with salt and pepper. Place the other half of the bread on top of the sandwich and lightly brush both sides of bread with the remaining 1 tablespoon olive oil. Press the sandwich in the panini press until the bread is golden and the cheese begins to melt, 3–4 minutes total.

If you use a non-stick griddle or cast-iron skillet, place another pan on top of the sandwiches while they're cooking, to give them a nice crispy exterior, and be sure to flip them over midway through cooking.

Cut into 4 sandwiches and eat while warm.

THE BEST GRILLED CHEESE SANDWICHES ◉

Serves 4 | Serve with Roasted Tomato Basil Soup (page 88)

There's nothing more comforting than a grilled cheese sandwich. I like to make mine with a combination of nutty Gruyère and sharp cheddar sandwiched between good grainy bread.

1 cup grated Gruyère cheese
1 cup grated white cheddar cheese
8 slices whole grain bread
1/4 cup extra-virgin olive oil

Preheat a panini press, non-stick griddle, or large cast-iron skillet. (For anything on the stovetop, preheat the pan over medium-high heat.)

In a small bowl, combine the cheeses.

On a cutting board, lay out the 8 slices of bread and brush 1 side of each with olive oil. Flip them over so they are oiled-side-down and top 4 of the slices with 1/4 cup of the cheese mixture. Top each with 1 of the remaining slices of bread, oiled-side-up.

Working in batches, press the sandwiches in the panini press until they are golden brown on both sides and the cheese is oozing out, 3–5 minutes.

If you use a non-stick griddle or cast-iron skillet, place another pan on top of the sandwiches while they're cooking, to give them a nice crispy exterior, and be sure to flip them over midway through cooking.

Cut each sandwich in half and serve.

BURGERS 3 WAYS:

Need I give a reason why burgers are one of the greatest culinary inventions of all times?! Nah, I think it's pretty self-explanatory. All of these burger recipes can be cooked indoors on grill pans, or outdoors on charcoal or gas grills. You may have to adjust the cooking times slightly to achieve the desired level of doneness.

....

BLACK & BLUE BURGERS

Serves 4

You'll never guess my secret to making really good burgers: Old Bay seasoning! I'm not sure why I decided to add a classic seafood seasoning to ground beef, but the result is pretty incredible. I personally love blue cheese on my burgers, but you could definitely substitute cheddar or another cheese.

1 1/2 pounds grass-fed ground beef

2 cloves garlic, minced

1 tablespoon Old Bay seasoning

1/4 cup chopped fresh flat-leaf parsley leaves

Fine sea salt and freshly ground black pepper

Canola oil, for brushing the pan

4 ounces blue cheese

2 tablespoons whole grain Dijon mustard

2 tablespoons ketchup

4 brioche buns, lightly toasted

Sliced tomatoes, thinly sliced red onion, and Bibb lettuce, for serving

In a large bowl, combine the ground beef, garlic, Old Bay seasoning, and parsley. Season to taste with salt and pepper. Form the mixture into 4 (1-inch-thick) patties. Season each burger with salt and pepper.

Heat a grill pan over medium-high heat, and brush lightly with canola oil. Grill the burgers over medium-high heat until a nice crust forms, about 4 minutes. Flip the burgers and continue cooking for another 3 minutes. Top each with 1 ounce of blue cheese and cook until the cheese softens and the burgers are medium-rare, 1–2 minutes. Remove the burgers to a plate and rest a few minutes before serving.

In a small bowl, whisk together the mustard and ketchup.

Serve on lightly toasted brioche buns with a dollop of Dijon-ketchup sauce and any combo of tomato, onion, and lettuce.

DO AHEAD: Make the burger mixture and form the patties 1 day ahead; cover tightly with plastic wrap and keep in the refrigerator. Let sit out 30 minutes before grilling, to bring to room temperature.

MONTEBUENA, "CUVÉE KPF" RIOJA, 2010 ($$)

Spain

$13.99

Try pairing this traditionally made Rioja with this flavor-packed burger. Smooth-tasting, with aromas of soft red fruit and leather, this excellent Spanish red works well with the grilled beef and blue cheese.

LEMONGRASS SALMON BURGERS WITH AVOCADO-WASABI SAUCE

Serves 4

These flavorful Asian-inspired salmon burgers are a nice, light alternative to the heavier red-meat variety. Lemongrass can usually be found in the produce aisle at many grocery stores, or in Asian markets.

SALMON BURGERS:

1 pound boneless, skinless salmon, diced

2 cloves garlic, minced

1 (1 1/2-inch) piece fresh ginger, peeled and grated (about 1 1/2 tablespoons)

1 tablespoon soy sauce

1 tablespoon grated lemon zest (1 lemon)

1 stalk lemongrass, trimmed and thinly sliced

3 green onions (white and green parts only), thinly sliced

1 large egg white

1/2 cup panko breadcrumbs

Fine sea salt and freshly ground black pepper

Canola oil, for brushing the pan

4 lemon wedges (1/2 lemon)

4 brioche buns, lightly toasted

Thinly sliced cucumber, for serving

AVOCADO-WASABI SAUCE:

1 avocado

1 jalapeño, seeded

2 tablespoons freshly squeezed lime juice, plus more to taste (1–2 limes)

1 teaspoon wasabi paste (or powder)

1/2 teaspoon soy sauce, plus more to taste

Fine sea salt and freshly ground black pepper

FOR THE SALMON BURGERS:

In a food processor, pulse together the salmon, garlic, ginger, soy sauce, lemon zest, lemongrass, and green onions. Add the egg white and panko breadcrumbs, season to taste with salt and pepper, and pulse until combined. Thoroughly clean the food processor. (If you don't have a food processor, finely chop the salmon then place it in a large bowl, add the garlic, ginger, soy sauce, lemon zest, lemongrass, and green onions, egg white, and panko breadcrumbs, season to taste with salt and pepper, and then stir to combine.) Form the salmon mixture into 4 (1-inch-thick) patties, wrap in plastic wrap, and refrigerate for 15 minutes.

FOR THE AVOCADO-WASABI SAUCE:

In the cleaned food processor, combine the avocado, jalapeño, lime juice, wasabi paste, and soy sauce and process until smooth. Taste the sauce and add more soy sauce or lime juice if desired; season to taste with salt and pepper. Chill until ready to use.

Heat a grill pan over medium-high heat, and brush with canola oil. Grill the salmon burgers until medium, about 3 minutes per side. Remove the burgers to a plate and squeeze the lemon wedges over them.

Serve on lightly toasted brioche buns with a dollop of avocado-wasabi sauce and thinly sliced cucumber.

France
Biodynamic
$19.99

CHÂTEAU DE LA SELVE, "ST RÉGIS" CÔTEAUX DE L'ARDÈCHE, 2012 ($$)

Floral and intoxicating, the Viognier grape doesn't suffer fools. La Selve's version, made from vineyards in the Northern Rhône, offers scents of white flowers and stone fruits, and enough power to hang tight with the salmon and wasabi.

TURKISH LAMB SLIDERS WITH TZATZIKI

Makes 8 sliders

These sliders are modeled after kofta, spicy Turkish meatballs that are typically served with tzatziki, a refreshing cucumber-yogurt dip.

TZATZIKI:

1/2 cucumber, peeled and seeded

1 tablespoon freshly squeezed lemon juice (1 lemon)

1 clove garlic, minced

1/2 teaspoon fine sea salt

1 cup Greek yogurt

1 tablespoon extra-virgin olive oil

2 tablespoon chopped fresh mint leaves

Fine sea salt and freshly ground black pepper

TURKISH LAMB SLIDERS:

2 cloves garlic, minced

1/2 teaspoon fine sea salt

1 pound ground lamb

2 tablespoons chopped fresh mint leaves

2 tablespoons chopped fresh flat-leaf parsley leaves

1 teaspoon ground cumin

1 teaspoon ground coriander

1/4 teaspoon ground cinnamon

1/4 teaspoon ground allspice

1/8 teaspoon cayenne

Fine sea salt and freshly ground black pepper

Canola oil, for brushing the pan

8 mini pitas, lightly toasted

Arugula leaves, for serving

FOR THE TZATZIKI:

Grate the cucumber on a box grater or finely chop. Place in a paper towel-lined colander and squeeze out any additional moisture.

Place the lemon juice in a small bowl. Place the garlic and salt on a cutting board and use the back of the fork to mash them into a paste. Add to the lemon juice and let sit for 5 minutes (this takes the bite out of the garlic). Pour into a medium bowl, add the cucumber, yogurt, olive oil, and mint and stir to combine. Season to taste with salt and pepper. Cover and let sit for an hour (or more) in the refrigerator to allow the flavors to combine. Store in an airtight container in the refrigerator for up to 2 days.

FOR THE TURKISH LAMB SLIDERS:

Place the garlic and salt on a cutting board and use the back of a fork to mash them into a paste. Transfer to a large bowl and add the lamb, mint, parsley, cumin, coriander, cinnamon, allspice, and cayenne. Season to taste with salt and pepper and stir gently to combine. Form the mixture into 8 meatballs. Let sit for 30 minutes to allow the flavors to combine.

Heat a grill pan over high heat and brush with canola oil. Flatten the lamb meatballs slightly to create 1-inch-thick patties. Grill until a nice crust forms, about 3 minutes. Flip the sliders and grill for an additional 2–3 minutes for medium. Transfer to a plate and let rest for a few minutes before serving.

Serve on mini toasted pitas with a dollop of tzatziki and a few arugula leaves.

Portugal
$9.99

ARCA NOVA, ROSÉ, VINHO VERDE, 2013 ($)

I love balancing the succulence of spiced lamb with a light and fruity—yet full-flavored—rosé. This one from Northern Portugal, made from Espadeiro grapes, answers the call. Portugal is a country to watch, still filled with great values that should make any wine- and food-lover swoon.

2 EASY NAAN PIZZAS:

When you're in a hurry and don't have time to make pizza dough, these individual naan pizzas make the perfect quick dinner or party appetizer. Just keep a package of whole wheat naan in the freezer at all times and you're good to go. There's no need to thaw the naan before tossing them in the oven.

TOMATO & MOZZARELLA PIZZAS

Makes 4 small pizzas

This has to be the world's easiest party appetizer (or main course, if you like). I love the classic tomato, mozzarella, and basil combo, but it's also fun to set out a variety of toppings and let each guest make their own.

4 whole wheat naan flatbreads

2 tablespoons extra-virgin olive oil

*8 ounces fresh buffalo or cow's milk mozzarella,
    thinly sliced*

1 cup halved yellow and red grape tomatoes

Fine sea salt and freshly ground black pepper

1/4 cup thinly sliced fresh basil leaves

Preheat the oven to 450°F. Line a baking sheet with aluminum foil.

Place the naan flatbreads on a baking sheet and brush with 1 tablespoon of the olive oil. Divide the mozzarella and tomatoes evenly among the 4 pizzas, and season to taste with salt and pepper.

Bake until the cheese is melted and the naan is golden and crisp around the edges, 8–10 minutes.

Drizzle the pizzas with the remaining olive oil and top with basil, then cut into pieces and serve.

WEINGUT KURT DARTING, "DÜRKHEIMER MICHELSBERG," RIESLING KABINETT, PFALZ, 2013 ($$)

Germany

Organic

$18.99

A pupil of Müller-Catoir, one of Germany's greatest estates, minimalist Kurt Darting is one of his country's best kept secrets. He produces wines that are soft and tasteful, and a great expression of their Pfalz terroir. His kabinett from the Michelsberg vineyard has lots of fruit, along with a lively acidity that balances the pizza's sweet tomato flavors.

RICOTTA & SHAVED ASPARAGUS PIZZAS

Makes 4 small pizzas

Tossed with a lemony vinaigrette, shaved, raw asparagus makes the most fabulous salad—and an even better topping for a pizza! Just crisp up your naan, smear with ricotta, top with the asparagus, and serve.

1 (1-pound) bunch large asparagus, woody ends trimmed

1/4 cup freshly grated Parmesan, plus more for garnishing

4 tablespoons extra-virgin olive oil, divided

2 teaspoons grated lemon zest, plus 2 tablespoons freshly squeezed lemon juice (2 lemons)

1/4 – 1/2 teaspoon red pepper flakes

Fine sea salt and freshly ground black pepper

4 whole wheat naan flatbreads

1 cup fresh ricotta

Preheat oven to 450°F.

Set the asparagus on a cutting board and, working with 1 asparagus spear at a time, slowly drag a vegetable peeler from the trimmed end to the tip to create thin strips of asparagus. (There will be oddly shaped pieces in the center of each stem that you can't use—either save for a soup or discard. It can be helpful to rotate the asparagus stalks as you go.) Shave all of the asparagus and place the strips in a large bowl. Add the Parmesan, 3 tablespoons of the olive oil, the lemon zest and juice, and the red pepper flakes and season to taste with salt and pepper.

Place the naan flatbreads on a baking sheet and brush with the remaining 1 tablespoon olive oil. Bake until brown and beginning to crisp, about 8 minutes.

Divide the ricotta evenly among the naan, leaving 1/2-inch border around the edges. Top each naan pizza with a generous heap of asparagus salad and top with additional grated Parmesan, if desired. Cut each pizza into pieces and serve.

VARIATION: I love serving this pizza with thin slices of prosciutto on top (or on a side plate so people can serve themselves). Also, if you're gluten-free, you can substitute a Glutino gluten-free pizza crust for the naan, or just serve this as a shaved asparagus salad.

LA SPINETTA, MOSCATO D'ASTI DOCG, BRICCO QUAGLIA, PIEDMONT, 2013 ($$)

Italy
Organic
$16.99

I love to pair asparagus-based dishes with vibrant, effervescent, and slightly sweet Moscato. Georgio Rivetti reinvented sparkling Moscato in the nineties, and still makes one of the most complete expressions of the variety. Asparagus is an extremely difficult vegetable to pair with wine, but this one does the job, and more.

SPELT PIZZA WITH RICOTTA & SPICY GREENS

Serves 4

Spelt is a nutty grain that makes a great alternative to wheat in breads, baked goods, and pizza crusts. Though it's not gluten-free, many people find spelt to be more easily digestible than traditional wheat. As for the topping, I adore the combination of creamy fresh ricotta and dark leafy greens sautéed with green onions and topped with lemon zest and red pepper flakes.

2/3 cup warm water

1 1/2 teaspoons active dry yeast

1 teaspoon honey

2 cups spelt flour

1 teaspoon fine sea salt

3 1/2 tablespoons extra-virgin olive oil, divided, plus more for drizzling and brushing the pan

6 green onions, thinly sliced

4 cups baby or regular kale, stems removed, thinly sliced

4 cups Swiss chard, stems removed, thinly sliced

Fine sea salt and freshly ground black pepper

1 cup fresh ricotta

1/4 teaspoon red pepper flakes

2 teaspoons grated lemon zest, or more to taste (1 lemon)

2 tablespoons freshly grated Pecorino (optional)

In a small bowl, whisk mix together the warm water, yeast, and honey. Let sit until foamy, about 10 minutes.

In a large bowl, whisk together the spelt flour and salt. Add the yeast mixture, along with 1 1/2 tablespoons olive oil and stir together until a sticky dough forms. Cover with plastic wrap and let rest in a warm spot until doubled in size, about 30 minutes.

Preheat the oven to 425°F and brush a baking sheet with a little olive oil.

Turn the pizza dough out on to a lightly floured work surface and knead the dough until smooth and pliable. If the dough is too sticky, add a little more flour to the dough—just sprinkle in a few extra tablespoonfuls at a time and gently knead it into the dough. Use a rolling pin to roll the dough into a rectangle that's nearly the size of your baking sheet.

Transfer the dough to the baking sheet, stretching it out slightly to cover the pan. Prick a few times with a fork, drizzle with olive oil, and sprinkle with sea salt. Bake in the middle of the oven until golden brown, 15–20 minutes.

While the dough is baking, in a large heavy-bottomed skillet, heat the remaining 2 tablespoons of olive oil over medium-high heat. Add the green onions and sauté, stirring occasionally, until softened, 4–5 minutes. Add the kale and Swiss chard and sauté, stirring occasionally, until wilted, 3–4 minutes. Season to taste with salt and pepper then use tongs to transfer the greens to a colander set in the sink and let drain.

When the pizza crust comes out of the oven, spread the ricotta over the entire surface, leaving a thin border around the edge. Spread the greens on top of the ricotta, then sprinkle with the pepper flakes, lemon zest, and pecorino, if using. Return to the oven and bake until warmed through, 3–4 minutes.

DO AHEAD: The pizza dough can be made 1 day in advance, covered in plastic, and refrigerated overnight. This will help it develop a better flavor. Bring to room temperature before proceeding.

QUPÉ, MARSANNE, SANTA YNEZ VALLEY, 2012 ($$)

I like to balance the fibrous feel of kale and Swiss chard with a rich and mouth-coating white such as
Marsanne or Roussanne—and this one has both! Bob Linquist has been making some of this country's best
Rhône varietals in California for over 30 years now. His wines still remain one of the best buys in the U.S.

USA
Biodynamic
$18.99

09 | SIMPLE SUPPERS

SPRING

Roasted Chicken with Lemon, Thyme & Shallots | 179

Cod with Brussels Sprouts, Bacon & Carrot Purée | 180

Seared Halibut with Pea-Fava Purée | 182

Roasted Salmon with Honey-Dijon Glaze | 185

SUMMER

Pesto Spaghetti with Tomatoes & Haricots Verts | 186

Parchment-Roasted Red Snapper with Tomatoes & Zucchini | 189

Garlicky Shrimp with Tomatoes & White Wine | 190

Grilled Skirt Steak with Chimichurri | 192

Grilled Fish Tacos with Avocado & Kale Slaw | 194

FALL

Whole-Roasted Branzini with Brussels Sprouts & Fingerlings | 199

Filet Mignon with Blue Cheese | 200

Quick Stir-Fry with Black Rice | 203

Crispy Pork Schnitzel with Mixed Greens | 204

Apricot-Dijon Chicken Thighs with Couscous | 206

WINTER

Roasted Pork Loin with Prosciutto & Rosemary-Fig Butter | 209

Spinach & Turkey Lasagna | 210

Lamb Ragù with Pappardelle | 212

Parmesan Polenta with Sausage Ragù | 215

Spaghetti Carbonara with Garlicky Greens | 216

GF

ROASTED CHICKEN WITH LEMON, THYME & SHALLOTS

Serves 4, with leftovers | Serve with Roasted Fingerling Potatoes (page 146) and Arugula, Radicchio & Fennel Salad (page 132)

I love making roast chicken, but it's kind of a pain to truss and carve the bird. I solve this problem by roasting individual pieces. It's less fuss, cooks more quickly, and has just as much flavor. Use the leftovers—if there are any—in salads or sandwiches.

1 (3- to 4-pound) farm chicken, cut into 8 pieces

1/3 cup freshly squeezed lemon juice (2 lemons)

1/4 cup extra-virgin olive oil

6 shallots, halved lengthwise and peeled

8 cloves garlic, smashed and peeled

10 sprigs fresh thyme

1 lemon, thinly sliced

Fine sea salt and freshly ground black pepper

1/2 cup dry white wine

3 tablespoons unsalted butter

Place the chicken, lemon juice, olive oil, shallots, garlic, and thyme in a large resealable plastic bag (or large bowl). Seal the bag (or cover the bowl with plastic wrap) and marinate at room temperature for 30 minutes, or up to 2 hours in the refrigerator.

Preheat the oven to 450°F.

Spread the chicken pieces out in a roasting pan. Drizzle with the marinade, including the shallots, garlic, and thyme. Add the lemon slices and season generously with salt and pepper.

Roast until the skin is golden and the internal temperature (taken at the thickest portion of the thigh and the breast) is 165°F, about 35–40 minutes. Raise the temperature to broil and broil the chicken until the skin is golden brown and slightly crisp, 2–3 minutes.

Transfer the chicken pieces, shallots, and lemon slices to a platter and cover loosely with foil. Add the white wine to the roasting pan and place over high heat. Let the pan juices and the wine simmer until reduced to about 1/4 cup, about 5 minutes. Whisk in the butter and season to taste with salt and pepper.

Pour the sauce over the chicken and serve immediately.

Store the chicken, in an airtight container in the refrigerator, for up to 2 days.

HENRY MARIONNET, "PREMIERE VENDANGE," TOURAINE ROUGE, 2012 ($$)

France
Biodynamic
$19.99

To accompany the roast chicken, try a slightly chilled Gamay from the heart of the Loire Valley. Fruit-forward, but a with nice grip that's unusual for Gamay, this wine (made by Henry Marionnet, a leader of the "natural" wine movement) works wonders here.

COD WITH BRUSSELS SPROUTS, BACON & CARROT PURÉE

DF / GF

Serves 4 | Serve with Endive Salad with Blue Cheese & Pears (page 129)

I love the bright colors and flavors in this dish. It may look a bit intimidating, but it's actually quite easy, especially if you break it into smaller steps. Make the carrot purée up to a day ahead and reheat it before serving. About 10 minutes before dinner, sauté the bacon and Brussels sprouts, sear the fish, and channel your inner Top Chef as you arrange everything on the plate.

5 cups peeled and coarsely chopped carrots
    (about 8 large carrots)

Fine sea salt and freshly ground black pepper

3 tablespoons extra-virgin olive oil, divided

3 slices nitrate-free bacon, chopped

1 cup Brussels sprout leaves

1/4 cup dry white wine

4 (4- to 5-ounce) pieces skin-on cod (or halibut)

In a medium pot, combine the carrots with just enough water to cover. Bring to a simmer and cook until the carrots are fork-tender, about 20 minutes. Drain the carrots in a colander, reserving about 1/2 cup of the cooking water. Transfer the carrots to a food processor, add a few tablespoons of the reserved cooking water, along with 1/2 teaspoon salt, and process until smooth. With the motor running, add 2 tablespoons of the olive oil in a slow, steady stream, blending until smooth. For a smoother purée, add additional water, 1 tablespoon at a time, and blend until smooth. (If you don't have a food processor, use a food mill, blender, or an immersion blender.) Season to taste with salt and pepper, cover, and keep warm.

Preheat the oven to 425°F.

In large skillet, cook the bacon over medium-high heat until beginning to brown, 4–5 minutes. Add the Brussels sprout leaves and sauté, stirring occasionally, until bright green and beginning to wilt, about 3 minutes. Add the white wine and simmer until evaporated, 2–3 minutes. Remove from the heat and season to taste with salt and pepper. Cover and keep warm.

Season both sides of the cod with salt and pepper. In a large non-stick ovenproof skillet, heat the remaining 1 tablespoon olive oil over medium-high heat until shimmering. Add the cod, skin-side down, and sear until a nice brown crust forms, 2–3 minutes. Flip the fish and place the pan in the oven to continue cooking until the fish is opaque and flakes easily, 4–5 minutes.

To serve, place about 1/2 cup of carrot puree in the center of each plate. Top with a piece of cod and spoon the Brussels sprout-bacon mixture over each piece of fish. Serve immediately.

France
Organic
$19.99

DOMAINE FRÉDÉRIC LORNET, PLOUSSARD, ARBOIS, 2009   ($$)

Light in color but packing a punch, the little-known Ploussard grape, from the Jura region of France, makes a nice pairing for this earthy cod dish. The Jura produces some of France's most interesting wines right now.

SEARED HALIBUT WITH PEA-FAVA PURÉE

DF / GF

Serves 4 | Serve with Whole-Roasted Carrots with Orange, Thyme & Garlic (page 149)

This dish was inspired by a recipe from cookbook author (and fellow La Varenne grad) Molly Stevens. I tweaked the recipe a bit—adding peas to the favas to make a lemon- and mint-spiked purée—and now I love making this for springtime dinner parties. To save time, shell and blanch the peas and favas the day before, make the purée the morning of, and then sear the fish just before serving.

PEA-FAVA BEAN PURÉE:

1 cup fresh shelled fava beans (1 1/2 pounds in the pod)

1 cup fresh shelled peas (1 pound in the pod)

2 tablespoons grated lemon zest,
 plus 1/4 cup freshly squeezed lemon juice

1/4 cup chopped fresh mint leaves

1/2 teaspoon red pepper flakes

1/4 cup extra-virgin olive oil

Fine sea salt and freshly ground black pepper

HALIBUT:

4 (4- to 5-ounce) skinless halibut fillets

Fine sea salt and freshly ground black pepper

2 tablespoons extra-virgin olive oil, plus more for serving

Chopped fresh mint leaves and lemon wedges, for serving

Coarse sea salt, for serving

FOR THE PEA-FAVA BEAN PURÉE:

Bring a medium pot of salted water to boil, and prepare a bowl of ice water. Add the fava beans to the boiling water and boil until the white skins are beginning to split, about 5 minutes. Use a slotted spoon to lift the fava beans from the boiling water and plunge them into the ice water to cool; reserve the boiling water. Let the fava beans sit in the ice water until cool, then use the slotted spoon to transfer them to a bowl; reserve the ice water. Slip off the white skins and discard. Place the fava beans in a food processor.

Add the peas to the pot of boiling water and cook until bright green and floating on the top of the water, about 1 minute. Use a slotted spoon to lift the peas from the boiling water and plunge them into the ice water. Let the peas sit in the ice water until cool, then use the slotted spoon to transfer them to the food processor. Add the lemon zest and juice, mint, and red pepper flakes and pulse several times to combine. Add the olive oil in a slow, steady stream, pulsing steadily to combine. Continue processing until the mixture is combined, but still slightly chunky. Season to taste with salt and pepper.

FOR THE HALIBUT:

Season the halibut on both sides with salt and pepper. In a large non-stick skillet, heat the 2 tablespoons olive oil over medium-high heat until nearly smoking. Place the halibut fillets carefully in the pan and cook until golden brown, 3–4 minutes. Flip the fillets, then reduce the heat to medium, and cook until opaque and beginning to flake, 2–3 minutes. Transfer to a plate and let sit for a few minutes before serving.

To serve, place a large dollop of pea-fava purée in the center of four plates and top with a piece of seared halibut. Squeeze the lemon wedges over the fish, sprinkle with mint, and drizzle with olive oil. Serve with a bowl of coarse sea salt for seasoning.

VARIATION: Swap out the halibut for jumbo scallops. Sear 12 scallops in a little olive oil over medium-high heat in a nonstick skillet for about 2 minutes per side—they are fantastic with the pea-fava purée!

AU BON CLIMAT, CHARDONNAY, SANTA BARBARA COUNTY, CALIFORNIA, 2012 ($$)

For over 30 years now, Jim Clendenen has been crafting some of California's finest wines. Never over the top, Clendenen's wines have an elegance and focus that's rarely surpassed. Halibut is one of my favorite types of fish, and pairs nicely with this delicious Chardonnay.

USA
Biodynamic
$16.99

DF / GF

ROASTED SALMON WITH HONEY-DIJON GLAZE

Serves 4 | Serve with Mediterranean Quinoa Salad with Roasted Summer Vegetables (page 119)

This is one of my go-to recipes when I'm cooking for a crowd, because it is so incredibly easy. I often double or even triple this recipe and serve it on a platter—it looks impressive and tastes even better. I prefer wild salmon, but if it's too expensive, I buy organic farmed salmon.

1 (1 1/4-pound) piece wild skin-on salmon

Fine sea salt and freshly ground black pepper

2 tablespoons whole grain Dijon mustard

2 tablespoons honey

1 tablespoon extra-virgin olive oil

1 lemon

6 – 8 sprigs fresh thyme

Preheat the oven to 450°F. Line a baking sheet with aluminum foil.

Arrange the salmon, skin-side-down, on the foil-lined baking sheet. Season to taste with salt and pepper.

In a small bowl, whisk together the mustard, honey, and olive oil. Pour the sauce over the salmon.

Cut the lemon in half crosswise, then cut 1 half into thin slices (reserve the extra lemon) and place them on top of the salmon. Arrange the thyme sprigs over the salmon and bake until just cooked through, 10 – 12 minutes. Remove the salmon from the oven and drizzle with the juice from the remaining lemon half. Arrange on a platter and serve.

MONTEBRUNO, PINOT NOIR, EOLA-AMITY HILLS, OREGON, 2012 ($$$)

USA
Biodynamic
$23.99

Joe Pedicini, the son of an old Italian wine family who settled in Oregon years ago, works exclusively with growers using sustainable or biodynamic farming practices. His Pinot Noir is soft and fruity, and with just the right ripeness to stand up to this salmon dish.

PESTO SPAGHETTI WITH TOMATOES & HARICOTS VERTS

Serves 4

This pasta is fantastic served warm, room temperature, or even chilled on a hot day. Everything can be made completely in advance and then tossed together right before serving. The leftovers are actually quite good for lunch the next day.

4 packed cups fresh basil

2 cloves garlic, peeled

1/2 cup pine nuts

1/2 tablespoon grated lemon zest,
    plus more for serving (1 lemon)

2 tablespoons freshly squeezed lemon juice
    (1 lemon)

1/2 cup freshly grated Pecorino, plus more for serving

1/2 cup extra-virgin olive oil, divided,
    plus more as needed

Fine sea salt and freshly ground black pepper

8 ounces haricots verts, halved

12 ounces dried spaghetti

2 cups halved yellow and red cherry tomatoes
    (about 1 pint)

In a food processor, pulse together the basil, garlic, pine nuts, lemon zest and juice. Add the 1/2 cup of Pecorino and 1/4 cup of the olive oil, and pulse to form a thick paste. With the motor running, add the remaining 1/4 cup olive oil in a slow, steady stream. If you want a thinner pesto, feel free to add another tablespoon of olive oil. Season to taste with salt and pepper.

Bring a large pot of salted water to boil, and prepare a bowl of ice water. Add the haricots verts to the boiling water and cook until bright green and still slightly crisp, 3–4 minutes. Use tongs to remove the beans and quickly plunge them into the ice water. Let the haricots verts sit until cool, then drain again.

Bring the water back to a boil, add the spaghetti, and cook, per the package directions, until al dente. Drain the pasta, reserving 1 cup of the pasta water.

Return the pasta to the pot. Add the pesto, haricots verts, tomatoes, and 1/2 cup of the reserved pasta water and stir to combine. (For a creamier sauce, add in a few more tablespoonfuls of pasta water.) Divide the pasta into bowls, and garnish with freshly grated Pecorino and lemon zest.

DO AHEAD: All the elements of this dish can be made earlier in the day. Purée the pesto, blanch the beans, cook the pasta (rinse it with cold water), and slice the tomatoes. Store everything in separate containers at room temperature (except the beans—keep those chilled!) until ready to toss together and serve.

Italy
Biodynamic
$19.99

CASTELLO DI AMA, ROSATO IGT, TOSCANA, 2013 ($$)

When one of the top estates in Chianti decides to try its hand at rosé, you can expect fireworks. Harvested from a 35-year-old vineyard, this wine delivers gentle aromas of dark cherries and wild strawberries that fold delicately around the lemon and tomato flavors of this delicious pasta.

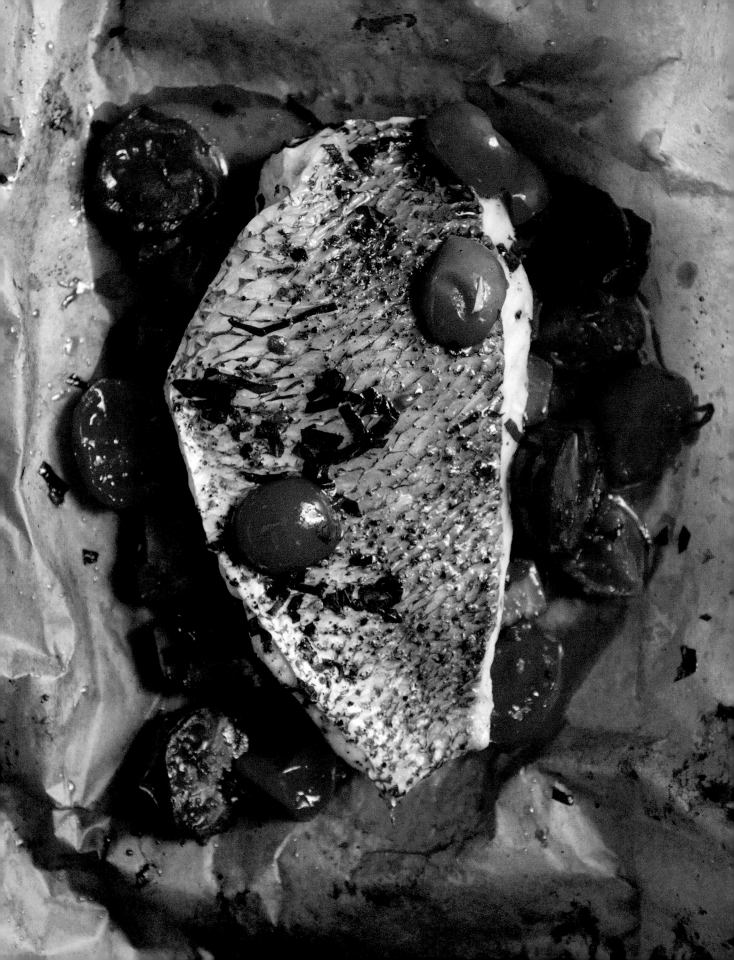

DF / GF

PARCHMENT-ROASTED RED SNAPPER WITH TOMATOES & ZUCCHINI

Serves 4 | Serve with Haricots Verts with Dijon Vinaigrette (page 124)

This is one of my favorite ways to prepare fish, because it's so light, easy, and flavorful—not to mention beautiful! You can make the parchment packages several hours in advance and keep them in the refrigerator until you're ready. Feel free to use any type of squash or zucchini, though baby zucchini are especially cute.

2 small summer squash, thinly sliced into rounds (I usually use a combination of zucchini and yellow squash)

4 tablespoons extra-virgin olive oil, divided, plus more for drizzling

Fine sea salt and freshly ground black pepper

4 (4-ounce) fillets red snapper (or other thin fillets, such as tile fish, tilapia, redfish, or trout)

20 red and yellow cherry or grape tomatoes, halved

1/2 cup dry white wine, divided

8 sprigs fresh thyme

2 cups cooked couscous,* for serving

Fresh, chopped basil, for garnish

Preheat the oven to 450°F. Tear off 4 sheets of parchment paper, each about the size of a standard sheet of paper.

Place 1 piece of parchment paper on a clean workspace. Arrange 1/4 of the zucchini slices in the center of the parchment, drizzle with 1 tablespoon of the olive oil, and season to taste with salt and pepper. Place one fish fillet on top. Scatter with 1/4 of the tomatoes, drizzle with 2 tablespoons of the wine, season to taste with salt and pepper, and top with 2 sprigs of thyme. Fold the parchment lengthwise over the fish, then roll each end towards the center. Press each side down to secure. Place the packet on a baking sheet and repeat with the remaining parchment and ingredients. If the parchment packages won't stay closed, you can flip them over. Bake until the snapper is cooked through and beginning to flake, about 10 minutes. Remove the fish from the oven and carefully open the parchment packages—beware of the steam!

To serve, spoon 1/2 cup couscous on each plate and top with zucchini and 1 snapper fillet, then spoon the tomatoes and any sauce from the parchment package on top of each. Garnish with fresh, chopped basil. Season with additional sea salt and drizzle with olive oil.

* Eliminate the couscous if you have a gluten sensitivity, or use quinoa instead.

KLOOF STREET, "OLD VINE," CHENIN BLANC, SWARTLAND, 2013 ($$)

South Africa

Organic

$18.99

With a new generation of farmers rediscovering its ancient vines, Swartland may be South Africa's most exciting wine region right now. This Chenin Blanc has aromas of citrus and quince paste that are soft enough not to overwhelm this gentle fish preparation.

GARLICKY SHRIMP WITH TOMATOES & WHITE WINE

DF / GF

Serves 4 | Serve with Spring Salad with Fava Beans, Peas & Radishes (page 110)

This dish was inspired by the garlicky shrimp at my favorite tapas bar in NYC, El Quinto Pino. Serve with plenty of couscous and good, crusty bread to soak up the sauce.

3 tablespoons extra-virgin olive oil,
    plus more for drizzling

3 – 4 cloves garlic, thinly sliced crosswise

2 shallots, thinly sliced crosswise

1 pint grape tomatoes, halved lengthwise

1 pound (about 16) large wild shrimp, cleaned and
    shells removed (with tails left in tact)

1/2 teaspoon red pepper flakes

2 – 3 teaspoons fresh thyme leaves,
    plus more sprigs for garnish

1 cup dry white wine

Fine sea salt and freshly ground black pepper

In a large sauté pan, heat the olive oil over medium-high heat. Add the garlic and shallots and sauté, stirring occasionally, until fragrant, about 1 minute. Add the tomatoes and sauté, stirring occasionally, until beginning to soften, 3 – 4 minutes. Add the shrimp, red pepper flakes, and thyme and sauté, stirring occasionally, until the shrimp are completely pink, about 3 minutes. Season to taste with salt and pepper. Add the white wine and bring to a boil. Reduce the heat to low and simmer until the liquid is reduced by half, 2 – 3 minutes. Taste and season with additional salt and pepper if necessary.

Arrange the shrimp on a warm platter or in a bowl, drizzle with olive oil, and garnish with thyme sprigs.

France
Organic
$13.99

CHÂTEAU MOURGUES DU GRÈS, "LES GALETS DORÉS," COSTIERES DE NIMES, 2013 ($$)

The Languedoc increasingly produces delicious, satisfying white wines made from Roussanne and Marsanne. This medium-bodied, broad-tasting white softens the intensity of the garlic and shallots without overpowering this light summer dish.

GRILLED SKIRT STEAK WITH CHIMICHURRI

DF / GF

Serves 4 | Serve with Detox Kale Salad (page 127)

I love skirt steak, because it's quick-cooking and extremely flavorful. It's especially good when rubbed with cumin, garlic, and lime, and then grilled and served with this herb-packed chimichurri sauce. While this is not a traditional chimichurri, it's similar to a roasted red pepper version I sampled years ago in Buenos Aires. It's great on steak, but it works well on just about any grilled meat, poultry, fish, or vegetables.

ROASTED RED PEPPER CHIMICHURRI:

4 ounces jarred roasted red peppers, drained

1/4 cup finely chopped red onion

2 cloves garlic, peeled

2 tablespoons freshly squeezed lemon juice (1 lemon)

1 1/2 tablespoons red wine vinegar

1/4 teaspoon red pepper flakes

1/4 cup fresh flat-leaf parsley leaves

1/4 cup fresh cilantro leaves

1/4 cup fresh mint leaves

1/4 cup fresh basil leaves

1/4 cup extra-virgin olive oil

Fine sea salt and freshly ground black pepper

CUMIN-RUBBED SKIRT STEAK:

1 1/2 pounds skirt steak, cut into 4 pieces

1 1/2 tablespoons ground cumin

3 cloves garlic, minced

2 tablespoons freshly squeezed lime juice (1 lime)

3 tablespoons extra-virgin olive oil

Fine sea salt and freshly ground black pepper

FOR THE ROASTED RED PEPPER CHIMICHURRI:

In a food processor, pulse together the roasted red peppers, red onion, garlic, lemon juice, red wine vinegar, and red pepper flakes. Add the parsley, cilantro, mint, and basil and pulse several more times to combine. With the processor running, add the olive oil in a slow, steady stream, blending until smooth. Season to taste with salt and pepper. Feel free to add more herbs, vinegar, or red pepper flakes according to your taste buds—this recipe is very adaptable! Cover the chimichurri and let it sit at room temperature for 1 hour before serving, so that the flavors have time to combine. Store, in an airtight container in the refrigerator, for up to 5 days.

FOR THE CUMIN-RUBBED SKIRT STEAK:

Place the skirt steak in a shallow (nonmetal) baking dish. Sprinkle with cumin and garlic, and drizzle with lime juice and 2 tablespoons of the olive oil. Using your hands, rub the seasoning into the meat until it's evenly coated. Cover and let sit for 30 minutes at room temperature or up to 2 hours in the refrigerator.

Brush the remaining 1 tablespoon of oil on a grill pan and heat over high heat until beginning to smoke. Pat the steaks dry and season on both sides with salt and pepper. Grill about 3–4 minutes per side for medium rare. (I don't recommend cooking skirt steak much longer or it will get tough.) The steaks should be rosy on the inside with a nice dark crust on the outside. Let the steaks rest for 5–10 minutes (preferably on a plate to catch the juices) then transfer to a cutting board.

To serve, thinly slice the meat against the grain and arrange on a platter, drizzled with the extra juices. Place the chimichurri in a bowl alongside.

France
Biodynamic
$12.99

CHÂTEAU DE LA SELVE, "PALISSAIRE," COTEAUX DE L'ARDÈCHE, 2011 ($)

Located in a beautiful national park near the Rhône Valley, this up-and-coming estate crafts superb value wines based on Syrah. The spicy and bacony flavors of this wine are an excellent match for the chimichurri sauce.

GRILLED FISH TACOS WITH AVOCADO & KALE SLAW

DF / GF

Serves 4 | Serve with Black Bean Spread (page 197)

There are a lot of elements in this dish, but the end result is worth it. The black bean spread and the slaw (minus the vinaigrette) can be made the day before. Marinate the red onions an hour ahead; assemble the other toppings while you marinate the fish, then toss it on the grill right before serving.

MARINATED RED ONION:

1/2 red onion, halved and thinly sliced into half-moons

1/2 cup red wine vinegar

GRILLED FISH:

*1/4 cup extra-virgin olive oil, plus more for brushing
    the grill pan and drizzling*

1 tablespoon chopped fresh cilantro leaves

1/2 teaspoon ground cumin

1/2 teaspoon chili powder

*1 teaspoon grated lime zest, plus 2 tablespoons
    freshly squeezed lime juice (1 lime)*

*2 (8-ounce) fillets Mahi-Mahi
    (or other firm, white-fleshed fish), skin removed*

Fine sea salt and freshly ground black pepper

Lime wedges, for serving

KALE SLAW:

1 packed cup thinly sliced kale

1 packed cup thinly sliced red cabbage

1 medium carrot, peeled and coarsely grated

3 tablespoons freshly squeezed orange juice (1 orange)

3 tablespoons extra-virgin olive oil

Fine sea salt and freshly ground black pepper

12 small corn tortillas, for serving

Avocado slices, for serving

Black Bean Spread (page 197), for serving

FOR THE MARINATED RED ONION:

In a medium bowl, stir together the red onion and red wine vinegar. Let sit for 1 hour and then drain; discard the vinegar.

FOR THE GRILLED FISH:

In a large, shallow glass bowl, whisk together the olive oil, cilantro, cumin, chili powder, and the lime zest and juice. Add the fish and stir to coat it in the marinade. Cover the bowl with plastic wrap and marinate, at room temperature, for 15–30 minutes.

Brush a grill pan with olive oil and place over high heat. Remove the fish from the marinade, pat it dry, and season both sides with salt and pepper. Grill the fish, flipping once, until white and flaky, about 4 minutes per side. Transfer to a platter, drizzle with olive oil, and garnish with lime wedges.

FOR THE KALE SLAW:

In a medium bowl, toss together the kale, cabbage, and carrot.

Pour the orange juice into a small bowl. Add 3 tablespoons of the olive oil in a slow, steady stream, whisking constantly. Drizzle over the slaw and toss until the vegetables are evenly coated. Season to taste with salt and pepper.

To serve, create a taco buffet, by setting out the platter of grilled fish, along with the kale slaw, a stack of warm corn tortillas (keep covered with a damp cloth so they don't dry out), and bowls of sliced avocados, black bean spread, and marinated red onions.

GOISOT, "EXOGYRA VIRGULA," SAUVIGNON DE SAINT-BRIS, 2013 ($$)

I love the freshness and pure mineral aromas of this Sauvignon Blanc paired with grilled fish tacos.
Made near Chablis in Northern Burgundy, this wine has been a fixture on all my wine lists for over
20 years now.

France
Biodynamic
$18.99

DF / GF / V ◉

BLACK BEAN SPREAD

Serves 4 | Serve with Grilled Fish Tacos with Avocado & Kale Slaw (page 194)

This spread is a good match for just about any type of taco or torta, but it also makes a terrific dip served with tortilla chips.

2 tablespoons extra-virgin olive oil, divided

1/2 red onion, finely chopped

2 cloves garlic, minced

1 teaspoon ground cumin

2 (14.5-ounce) cans black beans, rinsed and drained

Fine sea salt and freshly ground black pepper

3 sprigs fresh thyme

2 tablespoons chopped fresh cilantro leaves

2 tablespoons freshly squeezed lime juice (1 lime)

In a medium heavy-bottomed pot, heat 1 tablespoon of the olive oil over medium-high heat. Add the red onion and sauté, stirring occasionally, until translucent, 3–4 minutes. Add the garlic and sauté, stirring occasionally, until fragrant, about 1 minute. Add the cumin and beans and cook, stirring, until the beans are slightly softened, 2–3 minutes. Season to taste with salt and pepper. Add 1 cup of water and the thyme and bring to a boil. Reduce the heat to low and simmer, stirring occasionally, until thickened, 10–15 minutes. (The consistency should be like a chunky, thick paste.) Remove the thyme sprigs, stir in the cilantro and lime juice, season to taste with salt and pepper, and serve warm, drizzled with olive oil.

DO AHEAD: The beans can be made ahead and stored, in an airtight container in the refrigerator, for up to 2 days. Warm them over medium heat, stirring in a little water as needed to thin them slightly.

DF / GF

WHOLE-ROASTED BRANZINI WITH BRUSSELS SPROUTS & FINGERLINGS

Serves 4

This is one of those deceptively easy dishes, the kind that make you look like a total pro. Roasting fish whole makes for moist, flavorful flesh and wonderfully crisp skin—just warn your guests of tiny bones, which are unavoidable. Ask your fish market to clean and scale the fish for you.

1 pound Brussels sprouts, trimmed and halved

1 pound fingerling potatoes, halved lengthwise

2 tablespoons extra-virgin olive oil, plus more for drizzling

Fine sea salt and freshly ground black pepper

1 lemon

2 (1 1/2-pound) branzini, cleaned

20–25 sprigs fresh herbs such as thyme, rosemary, and marjoram

Place baking racks in the middle and lower levels of the oven and preheat the oven to 450°F. Line 2 baking sheets with aluminum foil.

Place the Brussels sprouts and potatoes on 1 foil-lined baking sheet, drizzle with 2 tablespoons of the olive oil, season to taste with salt and pepper, and toss to combine. Roast on the lower rack for 10 minutes.

While the Brussels sprouts and potatoes are roasting, thinly slice half of the lemon; reserve the other half. Use paper towels to pat the fish dry, inside and out. Season the cavities with salt and pepper and stuff each one with lemon slices and sprigs of fresh herbs. Arrange both fish on the second foil-lined baking sheet. Season to taste with salt and pepper and drizzle with a little olive oil.

Once the Brussels sprouts have been in the oven for 10 minutes, place the fish on the middle rack and roast until the flesh is flaky and cooked through and the Brussels sprouts and potatoes are crisp and golden brown, 20–25 minutes.

To debone the fish, use 2 forks to remove the top skin; discard the skin. Carefully transfer the top fillet to a warm serving platter. Lift out the backbone and ribs, then remove the bottom fillet and place it on the platter. (NOTE: A few small bones may remain.) Repeat with the other fish.

To serve, arrange the Brussels sprouts and potatoes on the platter with the fish. Squeeze with the remaining lemon half, drizzle with olive oil, season with additional salt, and garnish with additional fresh herbs.

COLD HEAVEN, "SANFORD & BENEDICT," VIOGNIER, SANTA RITA HILLS, 2012 ($$$)

USA
Biodynamic
$24.99

I love to pair branzino with this full-bodied, floral-scented California Viogner. It's one of the sexiest grapes in the wine world and the rich flavors easily stand up to this roasted fish with Brussels sprouts.

FILET MIGNON WITH BLUE CHEESE

GF

Serves 4 | Serve with Roasted Fingerling Potatoes (page 146) and a simple green salad

Make this special dish for a small dinner party. It's elegant, easy, and—with a bunch of candles and a good bottle of red wine—you can pretend you're at a bistro in Paris.

2 (8-ounce) filet steaks, halved to make 4 steaks

Fine sea salt and freshly ground black pepper

2 tablespoons unsalted butter

2 tablespoons extra-virgin olive oil

3 large sprigs fresh rosemary

2 cloves garlic, smashed and peeled

4 ounces blue cheese, crumbled (about 1 cup)

Chopped flat-leaf parsley leaves, for garnish

Remove the steaks from the refrigerator about 20 minutes before cooking, so the meat can come to room temperature.

Preheat the oven to 425°F.

Season the steaks on both sides with salt and pepper.

In a large heavy-bottomed oven-proof skillet, melt the butter and olive oil over medium-high heat. Add the rosemary and garlic and sauté, stirring occasionally, until fragrant, about 1 minute. Add the steaks and sear, flipping once, until a nice dark-brown crust forms on both sides, 2–3 minutes per side. Remove the garlic and rosemary, spoon some of the butter and oil over the steaks, and crumble the blue cheese on top. Transfer the pan to the oven and cook until the steaks reach the desired doneness, 2–5 minutes.

NOTE: The best way to test a steak's doneness is with a meat thermometer—I especially like the digital ones. For medium-rare steaks (bright pink interior), the internal temperature should be 125–130°F. For medium steaks (slightly pink), 135–140°F and for medium-well (no pink), 145–150°F. I like mine medium-rare, so I usually sear them for 3 minutes on the first side, 2 minutes on the second, and then finish them in the oven for about 3 more minutes.

Transfer the steaks to a plate and let rest for 5 minutes. Drizzle the steaks with any accumulated juices, sprinkle with chopped parsley, and serve with roasted potatoes and a mixed green salad.

France

$22.99

CHÂTEAU D'AURILHAC, HAUT MEDOC, BORDEAUX, 2009 ($$$)

The Bordeaux wines from 2009 are rich and flavorful, and this one—from a little known property in Northern Medoc—offers generous aromas of dark berries and mocha. A blend of Cabernet Sauvignon and Merlot, it has a nice structure that holds up well to the richness of the filet with blue cheese.

DF / V ⊙

QUICK STIR-FRY WITH BLACK RICE

Serves 4

I don't cook a lot of Asian dishes, but I love this healthy, simple stir-fry. And it's a great way to use up extra cooked rice—black or brown is fine. If you don't have a wok, a 10- to 12-inch non-stick skillet with sloping sides that are at least 2 inches high will also work.

2 tablespoons canola oil, divided

3 cloves garlic, minced

1 (2-inch) piece fresh ginger, peeled and grated (about 2 tablespoons)

2 medium carrots, peeled and cut into 1/4-inch-thick slices

3 tablespoons low-sodium soy sauce, divided

8 – 10 ounces shiitake mushrooms, trimmed and thinly sliced

2 teaspoons sesame oil, divided

4 packed cups baby spinach

Fine sea salt

2 cups cooked black or brown rice, cold

In a large wok, heat 1 tablespoon of the canola oil over medium-high heat. Add the garlic and ginger and stir-fry until fragrant, about 1 minute. Add the carrots and 1 tablespoon of soy sauce and stir-fry until the carrots start to soften, about 3 minutes. Add the mushrooms and 1 tablespoon soy sauce and stir-fry until the mushrooms start to soften, about 2 minutes. Drizzle in 1 teaspoon sesame oil and toss to coat. Transfer the mushrooms and carrots to a bowl; do not clean the wok.

Heat the remaining 1 tablespoon of canola oil in the same wok over medium-high heat. Add the spinach and stir-fry until just wilted, 1–2 minutes; season to taste with salt. Add the rice and mushroom-carrot mixture and stir to combine. Stir in the remaining 1 tablespoon soy sauce and the remaining 1 teaspoon sesame oil. Divide among 4 bowls and serve immediately.

VARIATION: Add in shredded, roasted chicken if you want some extra protein.

DOMAINE LA GRANGE TIPHAINE, "ROSA, ROSÉ, ROSAM," LOIRE VALLEY, NV ($$)

France

Natural

$14.99

Give this off-dry, naturally sparkling Loire Valley rosé a try. Bottled before all the sugars have stopped fermenting, and closed with a crown-cap, this wine is a perfect pairing for the stir-fry. La Grange Tiphaine is a leader of the natural wine movement in France.

CRISPY PORK SCHNITZEL WITH MIXED GREENS

DF

Serves 4

I first tried this dish in Germany, and immediately loved the combination of a crispy pork cutlet served with lemon wedges and a big green salad. If you don't have a meat tenderizer, use a rolling pin to flatten the pork chops.

PORK SCHNITZEL:

2 (5-ounce) boneless pork chops, halved lengthwise

1 cup red wine vinegar

2 large eggs

3/4 cup panko breadcrumbs

2 teaspoons freshly grated lemon zest (1 lemon)

2 teaspoons fresh thyme leaves

Fine sea salt and freshly ground black pepper

1/4 cup canola oil

Lemon wedges, for serving

MIXED GREENS:

6 packed cups mixed baby greens

2 tablespoons freshly squeezed lemon juice (1 lemon)

3 – 4 tablespoons extra-virgin olive oil

FOR THE PORK SCHNITZEL:

Place the pork in a resealable plastic bag (or a bowl), add the red wine vinegar, and seal the bag (or cover the bowl with plastic wrap). Place the pork in the refrigerator and marinate for 1–2 hours. (In a pinch, you can marinate it for 30 minutes).

Remove the pork from the red wine vinegar and use paper towels to pat it dry; discard the vinegar.

On a work surface, arrange the pork cutlets between 2 sheets of plastic wrap or wax paper. Use the flat side of a meat tenderizer to gently pound each piece to a 1/4-inch thickness.

In a shallow bowl, lightly beat the eggs.

In a second shallow bowl, combine the breadcrumbs, lemon zest, and thyme; season to taste with salt and pepper.

Dip 1 pork cutlet in the egg, letting any excess drip off, then dip it in the bread crumb mixture, making sure the entire cutlet is coated. Place the breaded pork cutlet on a plate and repeat with the remaining 3 cutlets. Chill the cutlets in the refrigerator for about 10 minutes to let the crumb mixture adhere to the meat.

In a large skillet, heat the canola oil over medium-high heat until almost smoking, about 2 minutes. Carefully add 2 cutlets to the pan and cook, flipping once, until golden brown and cooked through, about 3 minutes per side. Transfer to a paper-towel lined plate and cook the remaining 2 cutlets. Don't worry if the pork is a little rosy on the inside—that's OK!

FOR THE MIXED GREENS:

Place the salad greens in a large bowl.

Pour the lemon juice into a small bowl. Add the olive oil in a slow, steady stream, whisking constantly. Drizzle over the salad greens, season to taste with salt and pepper, and toss to combine.

To serve, place 1 cutlet on each plate, arrange the mixed greens alongside, and garnish with lemon wedges.

SCHLOSS GOBELSBURG, "GOBELSBURGER," GRÜNER VELTLINER, 2013 ($$)

A classic pairing, the softness of this Grüner blends well with the lemony flavors of the schnitzel. The Cistercian
monks, owners of this great estate, have fashioned one of Austria's best Grüner Veltliners for centuries.

Austria
Organic
$15.99

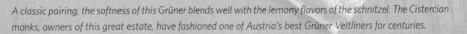

APRICOT-DIJON CHICKEN THIGHS WITH COUSCOUS

DF

Serves 4 | Serve with Roasted Broccoli (page 146)

I love the sweet-tangy combo of apricot and Dijon mustard in this dish, and it's so easy to throw together after work.

1/2 cup whole grain Dijon mustard

1/2 cup apricot jam

1 1/2 pounds boneless chicken thighs, fat trimmed

Fine sea salt and freshly ground black pepper

2 tablespoons extra-virgin olive oil, divided

6 sprigs fresh thyme

1 cup whole wheat couscous

Preheat the oven to 425°F. Line a baking sheet with aluminum foil.

In a large bowl, whisk together the mustard and the apricot jam. Add the chicken thighs and stir to completely coat the chicken. Season to taste with salt and pepper, stir, and let sit for a couple minutes at room temperature.

Pour the chicken mixture onto the foil-lined baking sheet and drizzle with 1 tablespoon of the olive oil. Scatter the thyme sprigs on top and roast until the internal temperature of the chicken (taken at the deepest portion of the thigh) reaches 165°F, about 20 minutes. Remove the chicken from the oven, cover with foil, and let rest for 5 minutes before serving.

While the chicken is resting, make the couscous: In a small pot, combine 1 cup of water, the remaining 1 tablespoon olive oil, and 1/2 teaspoon salt. Bring to a boil then add the couscous, cover, and remove from the heat. Let sit for 5 minutes, then fluff with a fork.

Serve the chicken over the couscous.

USA

Organic

$24.99

MATTHIASSON, ROSÉ, NAPA VALLEY, CALIFORNIA, 2013 ($$$)

This has been one of my favorite rosés of the past couple years. Light in alcohol (less than 12%) yet flavorful, with aromas of fresh peaches and apricots, it is a joy to drink, especially in a summer garden.

ROASTED PORK LOIN WITH PROSCIUTTO & ROSEMARY-FIG BUTTER

Serves 4 | Serve with Farro with Wild Mushrooms (page 135) and Haricots Verts with Dijon Vinaigrette (page 124)

I served this gorgeous roast for Christmas dinner last year and it was a huge hit. You can make the fig-rosemary butter several days in advance to save time.

4 tablespoons (1/2 stick) unsalted butter, room temperature

1/2 cup trimmed and finely chopped dried Black Mission figs

2 tablespoons finely chopped fresh rosemary, plus sprigs for garnish

1 clove garlic, minced

Fine sea salt and freshly ground black pepper

1 (1 1/2 – to 2-pound) pork loin

4 thin slices prosciutto

2 tablespoons extra-virgin olive oil

1/4 cup dry white wine

1/2 cup chicken stock

Preheat the oven to 375°F.

In a food processor, pulse together the butter, figs, rosemary, and garlic. Season to taste with salt and pepper.

Butterfly the pork loin: Make 1 long cut down the center so it lays flat like an open book. Season with salt and pepper and lay the prosciutto slices on top. Spoon the fig butter on top of the prosciutto, in a straight line down the center of the pork loin. Draw the two sides of the pork back together and tie tightly with butcher's twine.

In a large heavy-bottomed, oven-proof skillet, heat the oil over medium-high heat. Sear the pork, turning it, until browned on all sides, about 5 minutes total. Place the skillet in the oven and roast the pork until the internal temperature reaches 155°F, about 40–50 minutes (depending on the size of your pork loin). Transfer to a cutting board and let rest for 5–10 minutes.

While the pork is resting, add the white wine and chicken stock to the skillet and place over medium-high heat. Bring to a simmer, whisking in any burnt bits on the bottom of the pan, and continue simmering until reduced by half.

Cut the pork into 1/2-inch-thick slices and arrange on a serving platter. (NOTE: The pork will be rosy inside, but don't be alarmed! As long as the internal temperature is 155°F or above, you are perfectly safe.) Drizzle with the pan sauce and garnish with rosemary springs.

DOMAINE PIERRE USSEGLIO, CÔTES DU RHÔNE, 2011 ($$$)

Try a rich and flavorful gem from Southern France with this pork loin preparation. This Grenache blend offers notes of wild Provençal and Cassis that pair well with the rosemary-fig butter and the prosciutto.

France
Organic
$22.99

SPINACH & TURKEY LASAGNA

Serves 8, with leftovers | Serve with Arugula, Radicchio & Fennel Salad (page 132)

Lasagna is the ultimate cozy winter dish, but if often feels quite heavy. I lightened it up a bit by swapping ground turkey for the beef, adding a bunch of spinach, and making a homemade veggie-packed sauce. If you prefer, divide this dish into two smaller pans and take one to a neighbor (or freeze it for later).

5 tablespoons extra-virgin olive oil, divided

1/2 pound lean ground turkey

Fine sea salt and freshly ground black pepper

2 medium carrots, peeled and finely diced

2 ribs celery, finely diced

1 small onion, finely diced

4 cloves garlic, minced

1 (28-ounce) can whole peeled tomatoes with juices

1 tablespoon balsamic vinegar

1 teaspoon sugar

1/2 cup chopped fresh basil, divided

8 packed cups baby spinach

8 ounces fresh ricotta

8 – 10 no-boil lasagna noodles

2 cups shredded mozzarella

1 cup freshly grated Parmesan

In a large heavy-bottomed pot, heat 1 tablespoon of the olive oil over medium-high heat. Add the turkey and cook, using a wooden spoon to break up the meat, until it's browned and no more pink remains, 6 – 7 minutes. Season to taste with salt and pepper. Use a slotted spoon to transfer the turkey to a paper towel-lined plate to drain; do not clean the pot.

Add 2 tablespoons of the olive oil to the pot and place over medium-high heat. Add the carrots, celery, and onion and sauté, stirring occasionally, until the vegetables are softened and the onion is translucent, about 5 minutes. Add the garlic and sauté, stirring occasionally, until fragrant, about 1 minute. Crush the tomatoes with your hands (or a wooden spoon) and add them, along with the juices, to the pot. Season to taste with salt and pepper and bring to a boil. Reduce the heat and simmer, covered, for 30 – 45 minutes. Stir in the balsamic vinegar and sugar then taste the sauce, and season with additional salt and pepper if necessary. Stir in the turkey and 1/4 cup of the basil. Remove from the heat.

Preheat the oven to 350°F.

In a large skillet, heat 1 tablespoon of olive oil over medium-high heat. Add about 4 cups of the spinach and sauté, stirring occasionally, until wilted, about 3 minutes. Season to taste with salt and pepper then use tongs to transfer the spinach to a colander to drain. Repeat the process with the remaining 1 tablespoon olive oil and the remaining 4 cups spinach. Let cool slightly.

Transfer the wilted spinach to a medium bowl, add the ricotta and the remaining 1/4 cup basil and stir to combine. Season to taste with salt and pepper and set aside.

In a small bowl, stir together the mozzarella and Parmesan and set aside.

Spread a thin layer of turkey-tomato sauce on the bottom of a 9 x 13-inch ceramic or glass casserole dish. Arrange 1 layer of lasagna noodles on top of the sauce (it's OK if they overlap a bit). Spread half of the ricotta mixture over the noodles and sprinkle with 1 cup of the shredded cheese mixture. Spoon half of the sauce over the cheese. Repeat the layers—noodles, ricotta, cheese, and sauce—then top with the remaining cheese. (If you prefer to make 3 layers instead of 2, just create thinner layers and add an extra layer of noodles.) Cover with aluminum foil and bake for 30 minutes. Remove the foil and bake until the cheese is melted and the sauce is bubbling, about 15 minutes. If you want, broil the lasagna for 30 seconds to make the top a little bit crispy!

Leftover lasagna can be kept, in an airtight container in the refrigerator, for 2 days, and in fact it tastes almost better the second day. Warm in a 350°F oven until heated through, about 30 minutes.

DOMAINE JULIEN SUNIER, MORGON, BEAUJOLAIS, 2013 ($$$)

Julien Sunier is an upcoming young winemaker from Southern Burgundy, who makes fruit-driven, yet serious Gamay-based wines. This one has body and structure, but it is also fruity enough to play well with the lasagna.

France
Organic
$24.99

LAMB RAGÙ WITH PAPPARDELLE

Serves 4, with leftovers | Serve with Roasted Winter Squash with Kale & Pomegranate Seeds (page 140)

This dish was inspired by Andrew Carmellini's lamb ragù at Locanda Verde in New York's Tribeca neighborhood. It's perfect for feeding a crowd, as you can make the sauce a day or two ahead. I tripled the recipe one year for a New Year's Eve dinner party, and there wasn't a bite left.

2 tablespoons extra-virgin olive oil

2 small carrots, peeled and finely diced

2 ribs celery, finely diced

1 medium onion, finely diced

3 cloves garlic, minced

1 1/2 pounds ground lamb

2 teaspoons chopped fresh rosemary

2 teaspoons chopped fresh thyme

2 teaspoons ground coriander

1 teaspoon ground fennel

1 teaspoon ground cumin

Fine sea salt and freshly ground black pepper

3/4 cup dry red wine

1 (28-ounce) can whole peeled tomatoes with juices

1 1/2 cups chicken stock

1 1/2 tablespoons balsamic vinegar

1 pound fresh or dried pappardelle

Chopped fresh mint leaves and freshly grated Parmesan, for serving

In a large Dutch oven, heat the olive oil over medium-high heat. Add the carrots, celery, and onion and sauté, stirring occasionally, until the vegetables are softened and the onion is translucent, about 5 minutes. Add the garlic and sauté until fragrant, about 1 minute. Add the lamb, rosemary, thyme, coriander, fennel, and cumin and season to taste with salt and pepper. Cook, breaking up the lamb with a wooden spoon, until the meat is browned, 5–7 minutes. Spoon off any extra grease (I removed a good 1/2 cup or so). Add the red wine and simmer until evaporated, about 5 minutes. Crush the tomatoes with your hands (or a wooden spoon) and add them, along with their juices, and the chicken stock and bring to a boil. Reduce the heat to medium-low and simmer, partially covered, until the mixture begins to thicken, 30–45 minutes. Stir in the balsamic vinegar and season to taste with salt and pepper.

While the ragù is simmering, in a large pot of boiling salted water, cook the pasta, per the package directions, until al dente. Drain, shaking well.

Set aside 1 cup of the sauce. Add the pasta to the remaining sauce in the pot and toss to combine. Serve the pasta in bowls, topped with a dollop of the reserved sauce, chopped fresh mint, and plenty of grated Parmesan.

DO AHEAD: This sauce is even better the second day, so make it a day or two in advance and store, in an airtight container in the refrigerator. Just before serving, boil the pasta and gently reheat the ragù on the stovetop.

Italy

Organic

$22.99

PECCHENINO, "SIRI D'JERMU," DOLCETTO DI DOGLIANI DOC, PIEDMONT, 2011 ($$$)

Pecchenino is one of Piedmont's only estates to age their Dolcetto in new oak, enhancing its aging potential. This wine has hints of small red fruits, good acidity, and is well balanced with silky tannins, making it a nice foil for this rich ragù.

GF

PARMESAN POLENTA WITH SAUSAGE RAGÙ

Serves 4 | Serve with Broccoli Rabe with Pine Nuts & Golden Raisins (page 144)

In the depths of NYC winters, I love making this polenta and ragù for casual dinner parties. The sausage-filled ragù improves over time, so make it the day before, and reheat it just before serving. The polenta can also be made ahead, but you'll need to whisk in a bit of water to loosen it while you warm it on the stove.

SAUSAGE RAGÙ:

*2 all-natural, sweet or spicy Italian sausages
   (about 1/2 pound)*

1 small red onion, diced

3 cloves garlic, minced

1 (28-ounce) can whole peeled tomatoes with juices

1 1/2 tablespoons balsamic vinegar

1/4 cup finely chopped fresh basil leaves

Fine sea salt and freshly ground black pepper

PARMESAN POLENTA:

1 teaspoon fine sea salt

1 cup polenta (not quick-cooking) or yellow cornmeal

1 tablespoon extra-virgin olive oil

1/3 cup freshly grated Parmesan, plus more for garnish

FOR THE SAUSAGE RAGÙ:

Make a slit on one end of each sausage and slide the meat out of its casing.

In a large Dutch oven, cook the sausage over medium-high heat, breaking it up with a wooden spoon, until the meat is cooked through and no longer pink, about 8–10 minutes. Using a slotted spoon, transfer the sausage to a paper-towel lined plate and set aside. Do not clean the pot.

Pour out all but 1 tablespoon of the sausage grease from the pot. Add the onion and sauté, stirring occasionally, until translucent, 3–4 minutes. Add the garlic and sauté until fragrant, about 1 minute. Add the tomatoes, carefully crushing them with the back of a spoon, and bring to a boil. Reduce the heat to low and simmer, covered, until thickened, 20–25 minutes. Check the ragù periodically and if it seems dry, add some water. Add the sausage, balsamic vinegar, and basil and continue to simmer over low heat for 1–2 minutes. Remove from the heat and season to taste with salt and pepper.

Store, in an airtight container in the refrigerator, for up to 3 days, or freeze for up to 3 months.

FOR THE PARMESAN POLENTA:

In a medium heavy-bottomed saucepan, combine the salt with 4 cups of water and bring to a boil. Add the polenta in a slow, steady stream, whisking constantly. Continue to whisk the polenta for 2 minutes then reduce the heat to low. Cover and simmer for about 30 minutes, whisking every 10 minutes or so. The mixture should be thick and creamy, sort of like grits—if you're from the South you know what I mean! Remove from the heat and whisk in the olive oil and Parmesan. Season to taste with salt.

To serve, spoon the polenta into shallow bowls, top with the sausage ragù, and garnish with grated Parmesan.

TERRE NERE, ETNA ROSSO, SICILY, 2012 ($$)

Italy
Biodynamic
$19.99

Austere yet flavor-laden, this excellent wine, made from the little known Nerello Mascalese grape, is grown on the side of Mount Etna in Sicily. I like the match between its minerality and dried fruit aromas and the richness of the polenta and ragù.

SPAGHETTI CARBONARA WITH GARLICKY GREENS

Serves 4

This is one of my favorite winter pasta dishes, as it feels both hearty and healthy. The key is to mix everything together while the spaghetti is piping hot. Here's your game plan: While the water comes to a boil, prep all of the other ingredients, then once the pasta goes in the pot, cook the bacon and the greens. As soon as the spaghetti is al dente, drain, toss, and serve!

1/2 pound whole wheat spaghetti

5 slices nitrate-free bacon, cut into 1/2-inch pieces

1 clove garlic, minced

1/2 shallot, minced

5 packed cups dark greens, such as kale, spinach, or
*   Swiss chard, stems removed, torn into bite-size pieces*

Fine sea salt and freshly ground black pepper

1 large egg

1/2 cup freshly grated Parmesan,
*   plus more for garnishing*

Bring a large pot of salted water to boil. Add the pasta and cook, per the package directions, until al dente. Drain the pasta, reserving 1/2 cup of the pasta water.

While the pasta is cooking, in a large skillet, cook the bacon over medium-high heat until crisp, 5–6 minutes. Use a slotted spoon or tongs to transfer the bacon to a paper-towel-lined plate. Pour off all but 1 tablespoon of the bacon grease. Add the garlic and shallot and sauté, stirring occasionally, until fragrant, about 1 minute. Add the greens and sauté, stirring occasionally, until wilted, 2–3 minutes. Season to taste with salt and pepper.

In a small bowl, whisk together the egg and 1/2 cup of the Parmesan. Season to taste with pepper.

Return the drained pasta to the large pot, along with the egg and Parmesan mixture. Toss quickly with tongs, until all the pasta strands are evenly coated, adding the pasta liquid as needed to thin the sauce. Add the bacon and the greens, toss well to combine, and season with additional pepper, if desired. Divide the pasta among 4 bowls, top with Parmesan, and serve immediately.

Italy

Organic

$14.99

FRANCESCO BOSCHIS, LANGHE BARBERA, PIEDMONT, 2011 ($$)

Barbera is one of the great bargains of Italy, and deserves a place in any home cellar. Intense but delicate, with upfront tart fruit flavors, this red wine is from the heart of Piedmont, and is grown at high altitude. It offers a nice contrast for the garlicky greens.

10 | SWEETS

SPRING/SUMMER

Gluten-Free Almond Cake with Lavender Honey | 220

Strawberry-Rhubarb Crumbles | 223

Gluten-Free Banana Cupcakes with Cream Cheese Frosting | 224

Raspberry Crumble Bars | 227

Gluten-Free Key Lime Tart | 228

Strawberry Shortcakes | 230

Peach-Blackberry Crumble | 233

Strawberry Granita with Lime & Mint | 235

FALL/WINTER

Dark Chocolate Truffles | 236

Perfect Chocolate Chip Cookies | 238

Nutella-Shortbread Brownies | 240

Flourless Chocolate Cake with Raspberry Coulis | 243

Gingerbread Bundt Cake with Lemon Curd | 244

Bittersweet Chocolate Pudding Cakes | 247

Kahlúa-Butterscotch Puddings | 248

Cranberry-Pistachio Biscotti | 251

Ginger-Molasses Cookies | 253

Rosemary-Pecan Shortbread Bars | 254

Pumpkin Madeleines | 256

GLUTEN-FREE ALMOND CAKE WITH LAVENDER HONEY

DF / GF

Serves 8–10

This cake is so moist and flavorful, you'd never guess it was gluten- and dairy-free. It's also super-easy to make—even my husband, who doesn't cook or bake, was able to make this in 10 minutes! Though lavender honey is especially delicious, you can substitute any type of raw honey.

4 large eggs, room temperature, separated

1/2 cup lavender honey (or other raw honey)

1 teaspoon pure vanilla extract

1/2 teaspoon baking soda

1/2 teaspoon fine sea salt

1 3/4 cups almond meal

Powdered sugar, for dusting

*Fresh berries (and if you're not dairy free, Greek yogurt),
  for serving*

Preheat the oven to 350°F. Lightly spray a 9-inch springform pan with non-stick cooking spray or grease it with canola oil.

In a medium bowl, whisk together the egg yolks, honey, vanilla, baking soda, salt, and almond meal until smooth.

In the bowl of a stand mixer fitted with the whisk attachment, beat the egg whites on high until they are foamy and white, with soft (not stiff) peaks, about 2 minutes. Add to the egg yolk-almond meal mixture and gently fold them together until just combined.

Pour the mixture into the prepared pan and bake until the cake is golden brown and a toothpick inserted in the middle comes out clean, 25–30 minutes. Cool on a rack for 10 minutes, then carefully run a knife around the edges of the cake and remove the outer ring of the pan. Leave the cake on the rack to cool completely before serving.

Use a spatula to carefully remove the cake from the bottom of the pan and place it on a cake stand or plate. Dust with powdered sugar and serve with fresh berries and/or Greek yogurt.

This cake is definitely best when served on the day it's baked, but you can store any leftovers, wrapped tightly in plastic wrap at room temperature, for up to 1 day.

STRAWBERRY-RHUBARB CRUMBLES

Serves 4

In the spring and early summer, I make these crumbles all the time. The sweet-tart combo of strawberry and rhubarb, with a hint of orange, is just too good to resist.

1/2 cup whole wheat flour

3 tablespoons packed light brown sugar

1/8 teaspoon fine sea salt

3 tablespoons cold unsalted butter, cut into cubes

1/4 cup chopped walnuts

2 cups hulled and sliced strawberries
    (a little less than a pint)

1 1/2 cups (1 1/2-inch-thick) sliced rhubarb
    (about 4 medium stalks)

1/4 cup granulated sugar

2 teaspoons grated orange zest, plus 2 tablespoons
    freshly squeezed orange juice (1 orange)

Vanilla bean ice cream, for serving

Preheat the oven to 375°F. Lightly butter 4 (6-ounce) ramekins and place them on a baking sheet.

In a small bowl, whisk together the whole wheat flour, brown sugar, and salt. Add the butter and use your fingers to rub it into the flour mixture until crumbly, with pea-size bits of butter. Add the walnuts and toss to combine.

In a medium bowl, toss together the strawberries, rhubarb, granulated sugar, orange zest and juice. Divide evenly among the ramekins then sprinkle with the crumble topping.

Bake until the tops are golden brown and the fruit mixture is bubbling, about 25 minutes. Let cool at least 15–20 minutes. Serve warm with vanilla ice cream.

DO AHEAD: Assemble the crumbles earlier in the day, refrigerate, and then bake them during dinner, so they're warm for dessert.

GLUTEN-FREE BANANA CUPCAKES WITH CREAM CHEESE FROSTING

⊙ GF

Makes 24 cupcakes

My favorite cupcakes in the world are the banana ones with cream cheese frosting from Billy's Bakery in NYC. These taste pretty darn close, and they're gluten-free to boot. If you don't have a gluten sensitivity, you can make these with regular all-purpose flour.

BANANA CUPCAKES:

2 1/2 cups gluten-free all-purpose flour

1 teaspoon baking soda

3/4 teaspoon baking powder

3/4 teaspoon fine sea salt

1 1/2 cups mashed overripe bananas
    (about 3 large bananas)

3/4 cup buttermilk

1 1/2 teaspoons pure vanilla extract

3/4 cup (1 1/2 sticks) unsalted butter, room temperature

2 cups granulated sugar

3 large eggs, room temperature

1/2 cup bittersweet or semisweet chocolate chips
    (optional)

CREAM CHEESE FROSTING:

1 cup (2 sticks) unsalted butter, room temperature

4 cups powdered sugar, sifted

2 (8-ounce) packages cream cheese, cut into 16 cubes,
    room temperature

1 1/2 teaspoons pure vanilla extract

1/4 teaspoon fine sea salt

FOR THE BANANA CUPCAKES:

Preheat the oven to 350°F. Line 2 standard (12-cup) muffin tins with paper baking cups.

In a medium bowl, sift together the flour, baking soda, baking powder, and salt.

In a second medium bowl, stir together the mashed bananas, buttermilk, and vanilla.

In a stand mixer fitted with the paddle attachment, beat the butter on medium-high for 1 minute. Reduce the speed to medium and slowly add the granulated sugar then increase the speed to medium-high and beat until light and fluffy, about 2 minutes. Reduce the speed to medium and add the eggs, 1 at a time, beating after each addition. Reduce the speed to low and alternate adding the banana mixture and the flour mixture in 3 batches, starting with the bananas and waiting until each addition is blended before adding the next. Use a large rubber spatula to give the batter a final fold. Stir in the chocolate chips, if using.

Fill the paper cups (no more than!) 2/3 full. Bake until the cupcakes spring back when lightly pressed and a toothpick inserted in the center of 1 cupcake comes out clean, about 15 minutes. Cool on a rack for 10 minutes then turn the cupcakes out onto the rack and let cool completely.

FOR THE CREAM CHEESE FROSTING:

In a stand mixer fitted with the paddle attachment combine the butter and powdered sugar and beat on medium-high until light and fluffy, 2–3 minutes. Add the cream cheese, 1 piece at a time, beating after each addition. Add the vanilla and salt and beat until incorporated, about 1 minute.

To serve, spread or pipe about 1/4 cup Cream Cheese Frosting on each cupcake.

DO AHEAD: This recipe makes a lot of cupcakes, but you can easily freeze half of the un-iced cupcakes to enjoy at a later date. The frosting can be made up to 3 days in advance; bring to room temperature before frosting.

RASPBERRY CRUMBLE BARS

Makes 16 bars

Come summer, these raspberry crumble bars are on regular rotation at our house. To keep things simple, the shortbread dough that's used for the base doubles as a crunchy topping.

1 cup all-purpose flour

1/2 cup packed light brown sugar

1/2 teaspoon fine sea salt

1/2 cup (1 stick), plus 2 tablespoons cold unsalted butter, cut into cubes

3/4 cup old-fashioned rolled oats (not quick-cooking)

1/4 cup finely chopped pecans

1/3 cup raspberry jam

1 cup fresh raspberries

Preheat the oven to 375°F. Butter an 8 x 8-inch baking pan, or spray with non-stick cooking spray.

In a food processor, pulse together the flour, brown sugar, and salt. Add the butter and pulse until the mixture comes together to form a dough. Turn the dough out into a bowl and use your hands to gently knead in the oats and pecans.

Set aside 1/2 cup of the dough and press the rest into the bottom of the prepared pan. Spread the raspberry jam evenly over the dough, leaving a 1/4-inch-thick border. Arrange the raspberries over the jam, then sprinkle with clumps of the reserved 1/2 cup of dough.

Bake until the edges are golden brown, about 30 minutes. It will be a bit gooey in the center when you take it out of the oven, but it firms up as it cools. Set the pan on a rack to cool for at least 30 minutes before cutting.

Run a knife around the edges of the pan to loosen the bars. Make one cut down the center, rotate the pan and make a second cut down the center to create four large bars. Using a large spatula, lift the bars out onto a big cutting board and cut them into smaller squares.

These are best when served the day they are baked, but you can store any remaining bars, in an airtight container, layered with parchment, at room temperature, up to 1 day.

GLUTEN-FREE KEY LIME TART

Serves 8 – 10

Key Lime Pie is always a crowd-pleaser, so I thought it would be fun to create a gluten-free tart version. If you don't have a tart pan, you can definitely make this using a 9-inch pie plate. And if you can't find Key limes, feel free to use regular ones.

ALMOND-GRAHAM CRUST :

1 1/3 cups gluten-free graham cracker crumbs*

2/3 cup almond meal

4 tablespoons (1/2 stick) unsalted butter, melted

KEY LIME FILLING:

1 (14-ounce) can sweetened condensed milk

1/2 cup (fresh or bottled) Key lime juice

3 large egg yolks

1 tablespoon grated lime zest (1 lime)

Whipped cream and lime slices, for serving

FOR THE ALMOND-GRAHAM CRUST :

Preheat the oven to 350°F.

In a medium bowl, stir together the graham cracker crumbs, almond meal, and melted butter until evenly combined—the mixture will be crumbly. Sprinkle into an ungreased 10-inch tart pan with a removable bottom and use your hands to gently pat the crust evenly onto the bottom and up the sides of the pan. Bake in the middle of the oven until lightly browned, about 10 minutes. Cool on a rack for 15 minutes. Leave the oven set to 350°F.

FOR THE KEY LIME FILLING:

In a medium bowl, whisk together the sweetened condensed milk, Key lime juice, egg yolks, and lime zest until smooth. Pour into the fully cooled tart crust.

Bake until the center is set and the crust is golden brown, about 15 minutes. Set on a rack to cool completely, then refrigerate for several hours.

To serve, cut the tart into slices and serve chilled, with whipped cream and lime slices.

*To make graham cracker crumbs, pulse about 15 gluten-free graham crackers in a food processor until crushed into crumbs. Or, place the crackers in a resealable plastic bag and crush them with a rolling pin.

STRAWBERRY SHORTCAKES

Makes 10–12 shortcakes

Shortcakes, strawberries, and whipped cream—what's not to love? Bake the shortcakes the morning of the party, slice the strawberries and whip the cream a couple hours in advance, and then assemble these beauties just before serving.

SHORTCAKES:

2 1/2 cups all-purpose flour

5 tablespoons granulated sugar

1 tablespoon freshly grated orange zest (1 orange)

1 tablespoon baking powder

1/2 teaspoon fine sea salt

6 tablespoons (3/4 stick) cold unsalted butter,
　　cut into cubes

1 large egg, plus 1 large egg yolk

1 cup heavy whipping cream,
　　plus more for brushing shortcakes

Turbinado sugar or regular sugar, for sprinkling

STRAWBERRIES:

5 cups hulled and sliced strawberries (about 2 pounds)

1/4 cup granulated sugar

WHIPPED CREAM:

1 cup heavy whipping cream, chilled

2 tablespoons powdered sugar

FOR THE SHORTCAKES:

Preheat the oven to 400°F. Line a baking sheet with parchment paper.

In a food processor, pulse together the flour, granulated sugar, orange zest, baking powder, and salt. Add the butter and pulse until the mixture resembles a coarse meal. Transfer to a large bowl. (If you don't have a food processor, whisk the dry ingredients together then add the butter and use your fingers to quickly rub it into the flour mixture until only small, pea-size lumps remain.)

In a small bowl, whisk together the egg, egg yolk, and 1 cup cream. Add to the flour mixture and stir until just combined.

Turn the dough out onto a lightly floured surface and sprinkle with flour. Lightly flour your hands and knead the dough (it will be sticky) a couple of times until it has a consistent texture and color. Do not overwork the dough! The less you handle it, the more tender the shortcakes will be.

Pat or roll the dough into a 1 1/2-inch-thick circle. Dip a 2-inch biscuit cutter in flour and stamp out as many shortcakes as possible. Roll the scraps together and stamp out additional shortcakes. There should be 10–12 total. Place the shortcakes, about 1 inch apart, on the baking sheet. Brush the tops with a bit of cream and sprinkle with turbinado sugar.

Bake until the shortcakes are lightly golden and a toothpick inserted into the middle of a shortcake comes out clean, 15–20 minutes. Cool on a rack for 30 minutes. The shortcakes can sit at room temperature for several hours before serving.

FOR THE STRAWBERRIES:

In a large bowl, toss together the strawberries and sugar. Let sit at room temperature for 30–45 minutes or cover and refrigerate for several hours before serving.

FOR THE WHIPPED CREAM:

In the bowl of a stand mixer fitted with the whisk attachment, combine the heavy whipping cream and powdered sugar and beat until soft peaks form, 2–3 minutes.

To serve, cut the shortcakes in half horizontally and arrange the bottoms on dessert plates. Spread a few spoonfuls of the strawberries and their juices on each shortcake bottom then dollop with whipped cream. Top with the other shortcake halves, and serve.

DO AHEAD: These shortcakes are best when served the day they are baked, but to save time, you can measure out your ingredients the night before and store them separately, covered, in the refrigerator. Or, place the unbaked shortcakes on a baking sheet, cover with plastic wrap, and freeze for 45 minutes to an hour. Once frozen, place in a resealable plastic freezer bag and freeze until you're ready to bake them at a later date. When ready to bake, arrange the frozen shortcakes on a baking sheet, brush with cream, sprinkle with turbinado sugar, and bake as normal, adding a few minutes to the baking time.

PEACH-BLACKBERRY CRUMBLE

Serves 8–10

My friend Kelyn helped me develop this summery crumble, and her suggestions—like adding in lemon zest and vanilla extract—took it from good to extraordinary. Serve this with good-quality vanilla ice cream. It's also delicious eaten cold for breakfast, with Greek yogurt.

PEACH-BLACKBERRY FILLING:

5 cups sliced skin-on peaches
    (about 5 large ripe peaches)
2 pints fresh blackberries
1/4 cup all-purpose flour
1/4 cup granulated sugar
1 teaspoon cornstarch
1 teaspoon pure vanilla extract
1 teaspoon grated lemon zest and freshly squeezed
    lemon juice

OATMEAL CRUMBLE TOPPING:

1 cup all-purpose flour
1/2 cup old-fashioned rolled oats (not quick-cooking)
1/4 cup, plus 2 tablespoons packed light brown sugar
1/2 teaspoon fine sea salt
1/2 teaspoon ground cinnamon
1/2 cup (1 stick) unsalted butter, cut into small cubes
1/2 cup chopped pecans
Vanilla ice cream, for serving

FOR THE PEACH-BLACKBERRY FILLING:

Preheat the oven to 350°F. Butter a large 9 x 13-inch ceramic baking dish.

In a large bowl, toss together the peaches, blackberries, flour, granulated sugar, cornstarch, vanilla, lemon zest and juice. Pour into the prepared baking dish.

FOR THE OATMEAL CRUMBLE TOPPING:

In a second large bowl, stir together the flour, oats, brown sugar, salt, and cinnamon. Add the butter and use your fingers to rub it into the flour mixture until crumbly. Add the pecans with your fingers, and press the mixture together to create large clumps of topping. Sprinkle over the fruit and bake until bubbling and golden brown on top, 35–40 minutes. Set on a rack to cool slightly.

To serve, scoop into bowls and top with vanilla ice cream.

DO AHEAD: This can be made a day ahead and reheated in the oven. Let the crumble come to room temperature before putting it in the oven—otherwise the dish could break!

DF / GF / V ◉

STRAWBERRY GRANITA WITH LIME & MINT

Serves 4

I love serving this simple frozen treat when it's hot outside and I don't feel like turning on the oven. It's just barely sweet, and incredibly refreshing.

3 cups hulled and halved strawberries (a little over 1 pound)
1/4 cup finely chopped fresh mint leaves
3 tablespoons sugar
2 tablespoons grated lime zest, plus 1/2 cup freshly squeezed lime juice (4 limes)

In a blender, combine the strawberries, mint, sugar, lime juice and zest, and 1/2 cup water and blend until smooth. Pour into a 9 x 13-inch nonstick metal pan. Freeze until icy around the edges, about 30 minutes. Scrape the icy bits into the center and freeze for 1 more hour. Scrape with a fork until the granita is light and flaky. Cover and freeze overnight.

To serve, remove from the freezer and let sit for 5 minutes. Scrape again with a fork, and spoon the granita into shallow bowls or Champagne coupes.

DO AHEAD: The granita can be made up to 5 days ahead, and kept, wrapped in plastic, in the freezer until ready to serve.

DARK CHOCOLATE TRUFFLES

Makes about 28 truffles

Truffles are actually really easy to make; it just requires some organization. Be sure to read the recipe all the way through before getting started!

GANACHE:

8 ounces good-quality dark chocolate, finely chopped
(I prefer 60–70% and Valrhona is my favorite)

1 cup heavy cream

DIPPING CHOCOLATE AND TOPPINGS:

5 ounces good-quality dark chocolate, finely chopped
(I use 85% here)

Cocoa powder

Coarse sea salt (I use pink Hawaiian or rose sea salt)

Crushed roasted salted pistachios

FOR THE GANACHE:

Place the finely chopped dark chocolate in a large, heatproof bowl.

In a small saucepan, bring the cream to a simmer over low heat. Pour the hot cream over the chocolate. Cover with plastic wrap and let sit for 10 minutes. (Don't stir before 10 minutes—it will make the chocolate grainy!) Whisk the chocolate and cream until smooth then pour into a glass or metal loaf pan or a small casserole dish, and refrigerate for about 1 hour to harden the ganache. (Once the ganache has cooled a bit, you can cover it and even keep it chilled overnight.)

Line a baking sheet with parchment paper.

Remove the ganache from the refrigerator and use a mini ice cream scoop or a teaspoon to scoop roughly 1-inch (or slightly smaller) balls, then roll the balls in your hands to make them smooth. This gets really messy, so wearing plastic gloves helps! Otherwise, have a damp rag nearby so you can keep wiping off your hands as you go. As finished, arrange the truffles on the parchment-lined baking sheet, then place it in the freezer to firm up the truffles while you prep the dipping chocolate and toppings.

FOR THE DIPPING CHOCOLATE AND TOPPINGS:

Place the finely chopped dark chocolate in a microwave-safe bowl or container. With the power on 70%, microwave the chocolate in 30-second intervals, stirring between intervals. This will probably take about 3 minutes total. (Melting the chocolate this way will ensure it stays smooth for dipping.) Pour the melted chocolate into a shallow bowl.

Arrange your toppings in little bowls and line a second baking sheet with parchment paper.

Bring out your truffles and start the fun!

The simplest truffles to make are the cocoa-covered ones: Simply roll the ganache balls in cocoa powder and shake them to remove any excess.

For the rest, drop the ganache balls, 1 at a time, in the melted chocolate and use a fork to gently lift them out, letting the excess chocolate drip into the bowl. As finished, arrange the truffles on the parchment-lined baking sheet and sprinkle with a few grains of coarse sea salt. Or, roll the truffles in crushed pistachios after dipping them in the dark chocolate. Repeat with the remaining truffles, dipping chocolate, and toppings. Let the truffles harden at room temperature for at least 5 minutes.

Store truffles, in an airtight container at room temperature, for up to 3 days. The cocoa-covered ones have a tendency to get soft quickly, so I recommend keeping those in the refrigerator.

PERFECT CHOCOLATE CHIP COOKIES

Makes about 3 dozen cookies

This recipe is the result of my obsessive quest to create the perfect chocolate chip cookie: slightly crisp on the outside, gooey on the inside, and with plenty of chocolate chips and a touch of sea salt. My husband loves these cookies so much that I made hundreds of them—with help from a team of friends and family—as favors for our wedding.

1/2 cup (1 stick) unsalted butter

1/2 cup (1 stick) salted butter

1 cup packed light brown sugar

1/2 cup granulated sugar

1 large egg, plus 1 large egg yolk

1 tablespoon pure vanilla extract

2 1/4 cups all-purpose flour

1 teaspoon baking soda

1/2 teaspoon fine sea salt

1 (12-ounce) package semisweet or
    bittersweet chocolate chips

3/4 cup chopped walnuts (optional)

Soften both the salted and unsalted butter in the microwave (or on the stovetop) until nearly melted, about 1 minute. Let cool slightly then transfer to the bowl of a stand mixer fitted with the paddle attachment. Add both sugars, and beat on high until smooth and lightened in color, 2–3 minutes. Add the egg and the egg yolk and beat until fully combined. Add the vanilla and beat until fully combined.

In a medium bowl, whisk together the flour, baking soda, and salt. Add to the stand mixer and mix on low just until no flour streaks remain. Stir in the chocolate chips and walnuts, if using. Cover with plastic wrap and refrigerate at least 1 hour.

Preheat the oven to 350°F.

Drop tablespoonfuls of dough, about 2 inches apart, onto ungreased baking sheets.

Bake until the cookies are slightly brown and puffy, about 11 minutes for soft cookies and 13 for crisp ones. Set the baking sheets directly on the racks to cool for 10 minutes then place the cookies directly on the rack to cool completely. Eat one (or two or three!) warm with a glass of ice cold milk. Life doesn't get much better than this.

Store cookies, in an airtight container at room temperature, for up to 3 days.

NUTELLA-SHORTBREAD BROWNIES

Makes 24 brownies

These just might be the most decadent brownies of all time. I love cutting them into bite-size squares to serve at holiday cocktail parties—they're so rich that you really only need a taste. This recipe uses both salted and unsalted butter, so make sure you have both types on hand before you begin!

SALTED BUTTER SHORTBREAD:

2 cups all-purpose flour

1/2 cup packed light brown sugar

1/2 teaspoon fine sea salt

3/4 cup (1 1/2 sticks) salted butter, cut into small cubes

HAZELNUT NUTELLA BROWNIES:

1 cup (2 sticks) unsalted butter

8 ounces good-quality bittersweet chocolate,
    coarsely chopped

1 cup granulated sugar

4 large eggs

1 teaspoon pure vanilla extract

1/4 cup Nutella

3/4 cup all-purpose flour

1/2 teaspoon fine sea salt

1/2 cup whole roasted hazelnuts, skins removed

FOR THE SALTED BUTTER SHORTBREAD:

Preheat the oven to 350°F.

In the bowl of a food processor, combine the flour, brown sugar, and salt and pulse several times to combine. Add the salted butter and pulse until the mixture is full of pea-size lumps. (If you don't have a food processor, combine the mixture in a bowl. Using a knife and a fork, cut the salted butter into the flour to create pea-size lumps, or just use your fingers!) Sprinkle the mixture into an ungreased 9 x 13-inch baking pan and use your hands or a metal spatula to press the mixture evenly into the pan. Bake until golden, about 20 minutes. Transfer to a rack to cool. Keep the oven set to 350°F.

FOR THE HAZELNUT NUTELLA BROWNIES:

In a medium saucepan melt the unsalted butter over low heat, stirring occasionally. Remove from the heat, add the chocolate, and let sit for several minutes. Stir to fully melt the chocolate then transfer to the bowl of a stand mixer fitted with the paddle attachment. Add the granulated sugar and beat on medium until fully combined, about 2 minutes. Add the eggs, 1 at a time, beating after each addition. Add the vanilla and the Nutella and beat until fully combined.

In a small bowl, whisk together the flour and salt. Add to the chocolate mixture and mix on low just until no streaks remain. Stir in the hazelnuts. Pour the mixture over the shortbread and smooth the surface with a spatula.

Bake until a toothpick inserted in the center comes out with moist crumbs attached, 35 – 40 minutes. (The middle of the brownies may crack a bit—this is normal.) Set on a rack to cool completely.

Using a sharp knife, cut around the edges of the brownies to loosen them from the pan. With one hand on the bottom of the pan and one hand on the brownies, carefully flip the pan upside down onto a cutting board. Tap the pan a few times, then remove it—the brownies should be shortbread-side-up. Flip the brownies over so the shortbread side is on the cutting board and the brownies are on top. Dip a sharp knife in hot water and carefully cut the brownies into 24 bars, cleaning the knife and re-dipping it in the hot water between cuts. It's important to have a sharp knife for this process to cut through the hazelnuts!

Store the brownies, in an airtight container at room temperature, for up to 5 days or freeze up to 3 months.

GF ◉

FLOURLESS CHOCOLATE CAKE WITH RASPBERRY COULIS

Serves 8-10

I tasted flourless chocolate cake for the first time when I was living in France during college. It quickly became my favorite dinner party dessert, as it's so simple yet so impressive, and both the cake and the coulis can be made totally in advance. If you don't want to bother with the coulis, just serve the cake with a dollop of whipped cream and fresh raspberries.

FLOURLESS DARK CHOCOLATE CAKE:

1/2 cup (1 stick) unsalted butter

4 ounces good-quality bittersweet chocolate
(at least 70% cacao), coarsely chopped

3/4 cup sugar

3 large eggs

2 teaspoons pure vanilla extract
(or try a liqueur like Grand Marnier)

1/2 cup unsweetened natural cocoa powder,
plus more for dusting

RASPBERRY COULIS:

1 pound fresh raspberries or 1 (12-ounce) bag frozen
raspberries, thawed, plus more for serving

1/2 cup sugar

1 tablespoon freshly squeezed lemon juice (1 lemon)

FOR THE FLOURLESS DARK CHOCOLATE CAKE:

Preheat the oven to 375°F. Butter an 8-inch springform pan, place a round of parchment paper on the bottom, and butter the paper.

In a small saucepan, melt the butter over low heat, stirring occasionally. Add the chocolate, remove from the heat, and let sit for several minutes. Stir until the chocolate is fully melted then stir in the sugar and let cool for about 5 minutes. Add the eggs, 1 at a time, whisking after each addition. Whisk in the vanilla then sift the cocoa powder directly into the mixture and whisk to combine.

Pour into the prepared pan and bake until the top is set, 22–25 minutes. Cool the pan on a rack for 5 minutes, then run a knife around the edges and remove the sides. Let the cake cool completely, then gently turn it onto a serving platter and remove the parchment. Dust with cocoa powder, if desired.

FOR THE RASPBERRY COULIS:

In a medium saucepan, over medium heat, combine the raspberries, sugar, and 3 tablespoons water and cook, stirring frequently, until all the sugar has dissolved, about 5 minutes. Transfer to a blender, add the lemon juice, and purée until smooth. Pour through a fine-mesh strainer set over a medium bowl to remove the seeds.

To serve, cut the cake into 8–10 slices. Drizzle dessert plates with raspberry coulis and place slices of cake on top. Garnish with fresh raspberries.

DO AHEAD: The cake can be made 1–2 days ahead and kept, tightly wrapped, at room temperature. The sauce can be stored in an airtight container in the refrigerator, up to 5 days.

GINGERBREAD BUNDT CAKE WITH LEMON CURD

Serves 10 – 12

This cake is based on my friend Emily's grandmother's gingerbread recipe. It is dark, spicy, and absolutely delicious. Served with lemon curd, it's the ultimate winter dessert.

GINGERBREAD BUNDT CAKE:

1/2 cup (1 stick) unsalted butter, room temperature

1/2 cup packed dark brown sugar

1 large egg, lightly beaten

1 cup dark or blackstrap molasses

2 1/2 cups all-purpose flour

1 1/2 teaspoons baking soda

1/2 teaspoon fine sea salt

1 1/2 teaspoons ground ginger

1 teaspoon ground cinnamon

1/2 teaspoon ground cloves

1/4 teaspoon ground nutmeg

Powdered sugar, for dusting

LEMON CURD:

3 tablespoons grated lemon zest, plus 1/2 cup freshly squeezed lemon juice (3 lemons)

1/2 cup granulated sugar

3 large egg yolks

6 tablespoons unsalted butter, cut into cubes

FOR THE GINGERBREAD BUNDT CAKE:

Preheat the oven to 350°F. Spray a non-stick Bundt pan with non-stick cooking spray, grease with canola oil, or butter the pan and dust with flour.

In the bowl of a stand mixer fitted with the paddle attachment, combine the butter and brown sugar and beat on medium-high until light and fluffy, 2–3 minutes. Add the egg and beat until incorporated.

In a medium bowl, whisk the molasses with 1 cup water. Slowly pour this into the butter-sugar mixture and mix on low until combined.

In a large bowl, whisk together the flour, baking soda, salt, ginger, cinnamon, cloves, and nutmeg. Add to the butter-sugar mixture and mix on low until smooth.

Scrape the batter into the prepared pan. Bake until a toothpick inserted in the middle of the cake comes out with a few moist crumbs clinging to it, 45–50 minutes. Cool on a rack for 5–10 minutes, then carefully remove the cake from the pan and continue cooling directly on the rack.

FOR THE LEMON CURD:

In a medium heavy-bottomed saucepan, whisk together the lemon zest and juice, granulated sugar, and egg yolks. Add the butter and cook, over medium-low heat, whisking frequently until bubbles begin to appear on the surface of the curd and it's thick enough to hold the marks of the whisk, 6–8 minutes.

Transfer to a bowl, press plastic wrap directly on the surface of the curd, and chill at least 1 hour.

To serve, dust the cake with powdered sugar, slice, and drizzle with lemon curd.

DO AHEAD: This cake is even better the second day. It will keep, wrapped tightly in plastic wrap, at room temperature for 3–4 days. Lemon curd can be stored, in a jar or airtight container in the refrigerator, for up to a week.

GF ◉

BITTERSWEET CHOCOLATE PUDDING CAKES

Serves 4

For a chocolate lover like me, the darker, the better. I usually use Valrhona's 85% cacao bar in this recipe, because I find it perfectly compliments the lightly sweetened Grand Marnier whipped cream. Don't stress about serving these right out of the oven—in fact, I think they're better at room temperature.

1/2 cup (1 stick) unsalted butter

4 ounces good-quality bittersweet chocolate (preferably Valrhona), coarsely chopped

2 large eggs, plus 2 large egg yolks

1/4 cup granulated sugar

1 cup heavy whipping cream

1 tablespoon Grand Marnier (or other orange-flavored liqueur)

2 tablespoons powdered sugar

Chocolate shavings, for garnish

Preheat the oven to 450°F. Butter 4 (6-ounce) ramekins, sprinkle each with a bit of sugar, and place them on a baking tray.

In a small heavy-bottomed saucepan melt the butter over low heat, stirring occasionally. Remove from the heat, add the chocolate, and let sit for 2–3 minutes. Stir until the chocolate is completely melted. Let cool slightly.

In the bowl of a stand mixer fitted with the paddle attachment, combine the eggs, egg yolks, and granulated sugar and beat on medium until thickened and pale, 3–5 minutes. Slowly add the melted chocolate mixture, mixing on low until combined.

Divide the mixture evenly among the ramekins and bake until the centers are just beginning to set, about 8 minutes. The tops will puff up slightly like souffles but the centers will be deliciously soft and gooey. Cool on a rack for 10–15 minutes before serving, or bake before dinner and serve at room temperature.

In the clean bowl of a stand mixer fitted with the whisk attachment, combine the cream, Grand Marnier, and powdered sugar and beat on high until soft peaks form, about 3 minutes.

Arrange the ramekins on dessert plates then dollop the pudding cakes with whipped cream and garnish with chocolate shavings.

DO AHEAD: You can make the batter and fill the ramekins up to 1 day ahead. Cover with plastic wrap and refrigerate until ready to use. Bring to room temperature before baking.

KAHLÚA-BUTTERSCOTCH PUDDINGS

⊙ GF

Serves 6

SPICY PECANS:

2 teaspoons pure maple syrup

1 teaspoon packed dark brown sugar

1/4 teaspoon ground cinnamon

1/4 teaspoon cayenne

1 teaspoon extra-virgin olive oil

1 cup pecan halves

Fine sea salt

WHIPPED CREAM:

3/4 cup heavy whipping cream

1–2 tablespoons powdered sugar

1/2 teaspoon pure vanilla extract

KAHLÚA-BUTTERSCOTCH PUDDINGS:

2 1/2 cups whole milk

4 tablespoons (1/2 stick) unsalted butter

1 cup packed dark brown sugar

2 large egg yolks

3 tablespoons cornstarch

1/2 teaspoon fine sea salt

1 teaspoon pure vanilla extract

1 tablespoon Kahlúa (or other coffee-flavored liqueur)

FOR THE SPICY PECANS:

Preheat the oven to 350°F. Line a baking sheet with parchment paper.

In a small bowl, whisk together the maple syrup, brown sugar, cinnamon, and cayenne. Drizzle in the olive oil and whisk to combine. Add the pecans and stir to combine. Spread the nuts out onto the foil-lined baking sheet, season to taste with salt, and bake, stirring occasionally, until golden brown and beginning to crisp, 10–15 minutes. Cool on a rack until crisp and room temperature; roughly chop. Store in an airtight container for up to 1 week.

FOR THE KAHLÚA-BUTTERSCOTCH PUDDINGS:

In a small heavy-bottomed saucepan, bring the milk to a simmer over medium heat. Remove from the heat.

In a small skillet, melt the butter over medium heat, stirring frequently. Add the brown sugar, increase the heat to medium high, and cook, stirring constantly, until the mixture is golden brown and nutty smelling, 4–5 minutes. Keep a close eye on the mixture, as it can easily burn! Remove from the heat and very slowly pour the sugar mixture into the warm milk, whisking constantly. (If the mixture is clumpy, pour it through a fine-mesh strainer, pushing down on the solids with a spatula.)

Place the egg yolks in a heatproof medium bowl. Whisk in 1/2 cup of the milk mixture, then add the cornstarch and salt and whisk until dissolved. Pour in the remaining hot milk mixture, place over medium-high heat, and cook, whisking constantly, until the mixture thickens and begins to bubble, 3–4 minutes. (You'll know it's ready when the whisk leaves a trail through the pudding.) Remove from the heat and whisk in the vanilla and Kahlúa. Divide evenly among 6 small custard cups or ramekins. Place a piece of plastic wrap over each custard cup or ramekin, pressing it lightly onto the surface of the pudding, and chill overnight.

FOR THE WHIPPED CREAM:

In a stand mixer fitted with the whisk attachment, combine the heavy whipping cream, powdered sugar, and vanilla and beat until medium peaks form, 2–3 minutes.

To serve, remove the plastic wrap from the puddings then dollop each with whipped cream and sprinkle with spicy pecans. I like to put a small bowl of pecans on the table in case people want to add more—they're really good!

DO AHEAD: The puddings can be made 2–3 days in advance and kept, covered, in the refrigerator.

CRANBERRY-PISTACHIO BISCOTTI

Makes about 24 biscotti

These colorful biscotti, inspired by a Giada de Laurentiis recipe, will keep for a week in an airtight container, making them a perfect companion for a mid-afternoon cup of coffee.

2 cups all-purpose flour

1 1/2 teaspoons baking powder

1/4 teaspoon fine sea salt

1/2 cup (1 stick) unsalted butter, room temperature

1/2 cup sugar

1 teaspoon grated lemon zest (1 lemon)

1 teaspoon grated orange zest (1 orange)

2 large eggs

2/3 cup coarsely chopped, roasted, unsalted pistachios

2/3 cup dried cranberries

Preheat the oven to 350°F. Line a large baking sheet with parchment paper.

In a medium bowl, whisk together the flour, baking powder, and salt.

In the bowl of a stand mixer fitted with the paddle attachment, combine the butter, sugar, and lemon and orange zest and beat on medium until light and fluffy, about 2–3 minutes. Add the eggs, 1 at a time, beating after each addition. Reduce the speed to low and add the flour mixture, and beat until just combined. Stir in the pistachios and cranberries.

Turn the dough out onto the parchment-lined baking sheet and form it into a 13-inch long, 3-inch wide log. Bake until light golden, about 30 minutes. Set the baking sheet on a rack to cool for 30 minutes.

Transfer the biscotti log to a cutting board and use a sharp serrated knife to cut it on a diagonal into 1/2-inch-thick slices. Arrange the biscotti, cut side down, on the parchment-lined baking sheet. Bake, flipping once, until pale golden, 15–20 minutes. Transfer the biscotti to a rack and cool completely.

Store the biscotti, in an airtight container at room temperature, for up to 1 week.

GINGER-MOLASSES COOKIES

Makes 2 dozen cookies

These are the perfect winter treat, with a cup of milk or a mug of tea.

2 1/4 cups all-purpose flour

1 teaspoon baking soda

2 teaspoons ground ginger

1 teaspoon ground cinnamon

1/2 teaspoon ground cloves

1/4 teaspoon ground nutmeg

1/4 teaspoon fine sea salt

3/4 cup (1 1/2 sticks) unsalted butter,
    room temperature

1 cup packed dark brown sugar

1 large egg

1/4 cup molasses

1/4 cup raw or granulated sugar, for sprinkling

Preheat the oven to 350°F. Line 2 baking sheets with parchment paper.

In a medium bowl, whisk together the flour, baking soda, ginger, cinnamon, cloves, nutmeg, and salt.

In the bowl of a stand mixer, combine the butter and brown sugar and beat until light and fluffy, 2-3 minutes. Add the egg, molasses, and 1 tablespoon water and beat until smooth. Add the flour mixture and mix on low until just combined.

Place the sugar in a small bowl. Roll the dough into tablespoon-sized balls then roll them in the sugar until coated. Arrange the cookies, about 1 inch apart, on the parchment-lined baking sheets. With fingertips, press down lightly on each cookie.

Bake until golden and crisp around the edges, about 12 minutes. The cookies will still be soft in the middle when they come out of the oven. Set the baking sheets on racks to cool for 5 minutes then place the cookies directly on the rack to cool completely.

Store, in an airtight container at room temperature, for up to 3 days (though I highly doubt they will last that long!).

ROSEMARY-PECAN SHORTBREAD BARS

Make about 48 (1-inch) bars

I've made these pecan shortbread bars (adapted from an old *Gourmet* recipe) for years, but recently started adding chopped rosemary to the pecan mixture. The newer version is truly out-of-this-world. Note that this recipe uses both salted and unsalted butter.

SHORTBREAD BASE:

2 cups all-purpose flour

1/2 cup packed light brown sugar

1/4 teaspoon fine sea salt

3/4 cup (1 1/2 sticks) salted butter,
  cut into cubes

ROSEMARY-PECAN TOPPING:

1/2 cup (1 stick) unsalted butter

3/4 cup packed light brown sugar

1/3 cup raw honey

2 tablespoons heavy cream

2 cups roughly chopped pecans

2 teaspoons chopped fresh rosemary

FOR THE SHORTBREAD BASE:

Preheat the oven to 350°F.

In a food processor, combine the flour, brown sugar, and salt and pulse several times to combine. Add the salted butter and pulse until the mixture is full of pea-size lumps. (If you don't have a food processor, just combine the mixture in a bowl. Using a knife and fork, cut the salted butter into the flour to create pea-size lumps, or just use your fingers!)

Sprinkle the mixture into an ungreased 9 x 13-inch baking pan and use your hands or a metal spatula to press the mixture evenly into the pan.

Bake until golden, about 20 minutes. Transfer to a rack to cool. Keep the oven set to 350°F.

FOR THE ROSEMARY-PECAN TOPPING:

In a medium saucepan, melt the unsalted butter over medium heat. Add the sugar, honey, and cream, and bring to a simmer, stirring occasionally. Let simmer for 1 minute then stir in pecans and rosemary. Remove from the heat and pour the mixture over the shortbread, spreading evenly.

Bake until bubbling, about 20 minutes. Set on a rack and cool completely.

Once the bars are cool, use a knife to loosen the sides, then turn the entire pan out onto a cutting board. (This makes cutting much easier, and won't destroy your pan.) Use a sharp knife to cut 1-inch squares.

Store, in an airtight container at room temperature, for up to 1 week.

PUMPKIN MADELEINES

Makes 24 madeleines

I'm a huge pumpkin fan, and a huge madeleine fan. One day I asked myself: Why not combine these two loves? The result was revelatory. I keep a batch of these in the freezer throughout the fall to reheat as an afternoon treat.

2 large eggs

3/4 cups granulated sugar

1/2 cup canola oil

3/4 cup canned pumpkin purée (about half a 15-ounce can; not pumpkin pie filling)

1 cup all-purpose flour

1 teaspoon baking powder

1/2 teaspoon baking soda

1/4 teaspoon fine sea salt

1 teaspoon ground cinnamon*

1/4 teaspoon ground ginger

1/8 teaspoon ground nutmeg

1/8 teaspoon ground cloves

Powdered sugar, for dusting

Preheat the oven to 350°F. Spray a madeleine tin with non-stick cooking spray or grease it with butter or canola oil.

In the bowl of a stand mixer fitted with the paddle attachment, combine the eggs, granulated sugar, canola oil, and pumpkin purée and beat on medium until smooth, about 1 minute.

In a medium bowl, whisk together the flour, baking powder, baking soda, salt, cinnamon, ginger, nutmeg, and cloves. Add half of the flour mixture to the pumpkin mixture and mix on low until almost combined, 30 – 60 second. Add the rest of the flour mixture and mix on low until smooth.

Spoon tablespoonfuls of batter into the molds. (Do not overfill as they puff up while baking!)

Bake until golden and a toothpick inserted into the center of a madeleine comes out clean, about 10 minutes. Cool the tins on a rack for a few minutes, then turn the madeleines out onto the rack to cool completely. Dust with powdered sugar before serving.

Store madeleines, in an airtight container at room temperature, for up to 3 days. These also freeze really well. When you want something a little sweet with your coffee, pull one out and microwave it for a few seconds. It's like having a fresh-baked madeleine whenever you want!

*You can substitute 1 1/2 teaspoons of pumpkin pie spice for the cinnamon, ginger, nutmeg, and cloves.

11 | GATHERINGS

My biggest goal for this book is to inspire you to gather people around your table. Some of my best memories have taken place around the table, eating, drinking, laughing, and sharing stories with my friends and family. I want you to be able to create those same special moments with the ones you love.

People tell me all the time that they're intimidated to host a dinner party. They're not sure what to cook, worried about their lack of space, and afraid it will be a ton of work, so they end up going out to dinner (again). Honestly, I get it. I live in a 6th floor walkup apartment with a kitchen the size of a small bathroom. I never feel like I have the space—or time—to throw a dinner party. And yet my husband and I have people over all the time, and manage to make it work. I hope that in this section I can put your fears to rest, and make the whole dinner party process seem both doable and fun.

I've learned a couple of things from throwing dinner parties over the years, and there are four main keys to stress-free entertaining: *1) Plan ahead.* Develop a game plan for shopping and prep. *2) Do as much in advance as possible.* Saving things to the last minute will always cause panic. I make it my goal to be mostly done when the guests arrive, so I can enjoy spending time with them. *3) Throw perfection out the window.* Your friends are not expecting you to be the perfect hostess—they're expecting you to be YOU (who they already love and adore). And having a relaxed 'you' with a simplified menu is way better than any magazine-worthy spread. *4) Don't try to do it all.* Enlist the help of friends. Everyone always asks how they can help, so let them! Whether it's bringing a bottle of wine, an appetizer, a dessert, or a bouquet of flowers, contributions from friends not only lighten your workload, but they also make people feel like they're a special part of the evening.

Here are a few more helpful tips...

GUEST LIST

• **Mix it up.** When hosting dinner parties, I love to bring different sets of friends together—some of Brandon's, some of mine, and some of ours—and watch the worlds collide. As important as the food and the ambiance are, it's the people that make a dinner party. Though I may recall a certain dish the next day (if it was really good), what will linger for weeks and months are stories told, laughter shared, and new friendships formed.

- **Use place cards.** It may seem formal, but I actually like to decide in advance where people sit, and create little name cards. I find that the conversation flows better when there's some intention about who sits where, and who you think would enjoy talking. New relationships are formed this way, and it avoids old friends sitting at one end of the table, while all the newbies sit awkwardly at the other end.

- **Ask questions.** As an icebreaker, I love having a fun question prepared to ask the entire table like, "What would you do if you weren't working in your current job?" or "What celebrity do people say you look like?" Another option is to just do little intros, where everyone says who they are, how they know the host, and what they're looking forward to in their particular season of life. My favorite dinner parties are the ones where the whole table gets in on a conversation.

MENU-PLANNING

- **Keep it simple.** There may be ten fabulous new recipes you are dying to try, but a dinner party is not the time to try them all. Feel free to try one new thing, but keep the other dishes no-brainers so you know exactly how they'll turn out.

- **Serve one course.** I'm a huge fan of one-pot dinners, especially in the fall and winter. Lamb tagine (page 105), sausage ragù (page 215), or a big pot of chili (page 98) can be made in advance and reheated when everyone arrives. And best of all, they can be dished out right from the pot, and served with a green salad and some crusty bread to round things out. In the summertime keep it simple and serve a no-cook spread of Caprese salad (page 115), watermelon feta skewers (page 77), and arugula salad with favas and peas (page 111).

- **Be strategic.** Think about which dishes can be made in advance (the more, the better!), as well as which ones go in the oven, cook on the stove top, or need to be chilled. Try to have a balance of hot and cold dishes so you're not sweating (literally) waiting for everything to come out of the oven at the same time.

- **Family-style, buffet, or plated?** Consider how you want to serve each dish. Usually I keep it simple and just set up a buffet so guests can serve themselves. But if I want to get really fancy (which sometimes I like to do!) I'll plate each dish, and serve it restaurant-style. I know that's a bit fussy, but it allows me to style the food exactly the way I envision it.

- **Go shopping.** There is no shame in buying a few things already made. If you're making the main course, pick up a dessert from a bakery. Or assemble a cheese platter instead of making hors d'oeuvres. Enjoying your guests is the goal, and they would rather be with you than have you stuck in the kitchen all night.

TABLE + DECOR

- **Set your table in advance.** Not only is this one less thing you have to worry about later in the day, but it also helps get you in the dinner party mood. Plus, in the event that you're short on silverware (or glasses or plates), you'll have time to either run out and get a few more, or ask one of your guests to bring extra.

- **Use cloth napkins.** I'm a big fan of cloth napkins, but I go through so many that I don't buy anything expensive. IKEA has simple, striped dishtowels that make great napkins. I also buy packs of inexpensive plain white ones from Bed, Bath, and Beyond.

- **Create simple place-settings.** My stylist friend Jenn Elliott Blake showed me this super-simple (and adorable) place-setting: place a folded napkin on a plate and top with silverware, tied with a piece of twine. So easy, but super-cute.

- **Keep water on the table.** I fill old milk bottles and glass carafes (no need for them to match!) and keep them on the table during a dinner party so I don't have to keep hopping up and down to refill water glasses. Vintage bottles are beautiful, but almost anything will do—you can even use recycled wine bottles.

- **Make mini bouquets.** I love flowers, but I avoid tall arrangements on the table that block conversation. My mom gave me some of my great grandmother's perfume bottles and they make beautiful little vases. I'll put a single flower in each and line the table with these mismatched vintage arrangements. And I love to put one in the bathroom as well.

- **Put your menu on display.** I have a chalkboard hanging in the kitchen that I write the menu on, but sometimes it's fun to have hand-written menu cards at everyone's place setting.

PRE-PARTY

- **Set the ambiance.** Light some candles, dim the lamps (which helps disguise those areas you didn't have time to dust!), and have a great playlist going when guests arrive. I'm a sucker for jazz—Ella Fitzgerald, Miles

A simple and adorable place-setting, styled by my friend Jenn Elliott Blake; PHOTO BY SIGNE BIRCK (RIGHT)

Davis, John Coltrane, Diana Krall, and St. Germain are all favorites of mine for dinner parties.

• **Get yourself ready.** An hour before the party, stop what you're doing and freshen up. Whether that means showering or just slipping on a dress or touching up your makeup, don't save this until the last minute! You can always do final food prep once guests arrive, and you don't want to greet your friends in a towel with wet hair. (Trust me...I've done it!)

• **Have drinks and snacks ready.** This one is essential. As long as everyone has something to sip and something to nibble on when they arrive, they're fine hanging out in the living room while I put the finishing touches on the meal. Lucky for me, we have an open kitchen that faces the living room, so I can still be

part of the party while I'm cooking. And your hors d' oeuvres don't need to be elaborate. Make Spicy Maple-Rosemary Cocktail Nuts (page 73), Citrus-Marinated Olives (page 70), or Crudités with Lemon-Parsley Tahini Dip (page 74).

• **Enlist a friend.** Ask someone to come early and help you with last-minute stuff. Inevitably, I'm running around at the last minute trying to do 20 things. A friend can help light candles, put out ice, turn on the music, assemble crostini, or any other thing you didn't get around to doing.

• **Relax.** Keep a bottle of bubbly in the fridge and have a glass before guests arrive. Take a deep breath and remember to have fun—otherwise, why bother hosting?

MENU IDEAS

Here are a few menu ideas for your next brunch or dinner party gathering.

BRUNCH

Vegetarian Brunch Buffet

29   Crunchy Maple-Pecan Granola with Greek Yogurt
     & Berries
34   Mini Frittatas with Spinach, Goat Cheese &
     Roasted Tomatoes
44   Orange Zest Scones with Strawberry-Rhubarb
     Compote
136 Citrus Salad with Arugula & Ricotta Salata

Casual Brunch Buffet

33   Crustless Quiche Lorraine
39   Rosemary-Parmesan Biscuits with Fig Jam
     & Prosciutto
36   Sour Cream-Banana Muffins
     Fruit Salad

DINNER
(SPRING)

Classic French Bistro

110 Spring Salad with Fava Beans, Peas & Radishes
179 Roasted Chicken with Lemon, Thyme & Shallots
146 Roasted Fingerling Potatoes
220 Gluten-Free Almond Cake with Lavender Honey

Spring Dinner Party

109 Salade de Chèvre Chaud
     (Warm Goat Cheese Salad)
182 Seared Halibut with Pea-Fava Purée
149 Whole-Roasted Carrots with Orange,
     Thyme & Garlic
223 Strawberry-Rhubarb Crumbles

(SUMMER)

Summer Cookout

153 Avocado & Ricotta Toasts
192 Grilled Skirt Steak with Chimichurri
127 Detox Kale Salad
233 Peach-Blackberry Crumble

Light & Summery

77   Watermelon, Feta & Mint Skewers
189 Parchment-Roasted Red Snapper with Tomatoes
     & Zucchini
     Couscous
230 Strawberry Shortcakes

(FALL)

Fall Gluten-Free

74   Crudités with Lemon-Parsley Tahini Dip
179 Roasted Salmon with Honey-Dijon Glaze
130 Red Quinoa Salad with Butternut Squash & Spinach
243 Flourless Chocolate Cake with Raspberry Coulis

Elegant Fall Dinner Party

66   Crostini with Brie & Sundried Tomato-Walnut
     Tapenade
199 Whole-Roasted Branzini with Brussels Sprouts
     & Fingerlings
149 Whole-Roasted Carrots with Orange, Thyme
     & Garlic
248 Kalhúa-Butterscotch Puddings

(WINTER)

Winter Italian Comfort Food

70   Citrus-Marinated Olives
210 Spinach & Turkey Lasagna
132 Arugula, Radicchio & Fennel Salad
247 Bittersweet Chocolate Pudding Cakes

Cozy Winter Dinner

136 Citrus Salad with Arugula & Ricotta Salata
215 Parmesan Polenta with Sausage Ragù
144 Broccoli Rabe with Pine Nuts & Golden Raisins
244 Gingerbread Bundt Cake with Lemon Curd

Holiday Feast

44   Butternut Squash Soup with Spiced Pears
209 Roasted Pork Loin with Prosciutto &
     Rosemary-Fig Butter
135 Farro with Wild Mushrooms
124 Haricots Verts with Dijon Vinaigrette
240 Nutella-Shortbread Brownies

ANYTIME

Quick & Easy Supper with Friends

59   Bacon-Wrapped Dates with Almonds
206 Apricot-Dijon Chicken Thighs with Couscous
146 Simple Roasted Broccoli (or Cauliflower)
254 Rosemary-Pecan Shortbread Bars

Vegan Feast

74   Crudités with Lemon-Parsley Tahini Dip
102 Tomato-Chickpea Curry with Kale
     Brown Rice
235 Strawberry Granita with Lime & Mint

A gnocchi-themed dinner party around the yellow table. **PHOTO BY ERIC RYAN ANDERSON (RIGHT)**

ACKNOWLEDGMENTS

(LEFT) Dynamic duo: Anna Watson Carl & Signe Birck. **PHOTO BY ERIC RYAN ANDERSON**

It has been such a joy, not only getting to write this book, but also having the opportunity to collaborate with so many incredible folks. This project has taught me (among many other things) that dreams rarely happen in isolation—it truly takes a village. This book would never have been possible without the time, talents, generosity, and enthusiasm of the following people.

A GIGANTIC THANK YOU TO:

My dear husband, Brandon, who helped me find the courage to take the leap of faith to start this book, and who has been a constant source of encouragement, support, and inspiration, every step of the way. I love you.

My cookbook dream team: Signe Birck, for agreeing to shoot this cookbook in my walk-up apartment, in the dead of winter, in the most hilariously low-budget conditions. Your photos are stunning, and make my food look far better than I could have ever imagined. Jean-Luc Le Dû, for creating such fantastic wine pairings—I am beyond grateful to have your passion for wine woven into the book. My incredible designer Katie King Rumford: wow. The designs for this book go above and beyond my wildest dreams. Lauren Salkeld, my wonderful editor, for being everything that I'm not: organized, detail-oriented, and deadline-focused. Were it not for your expertise, enthusiasm, and saint-like patience, this book would still be a pile of untested

recipe drafts! Elise Inman, my amazing intern; whether schlepping groceries and props up the stairs, prepping for photo shoots, or driving across the country with me, your sense of humor (and cat stories!) made this project a lot more fun. Dana Tanamachi-Williams, for designing such a killer logo. I am in awe. Eric Ryan Anderson, for not laughing when I told you about this project, and for agreeing to shoot a stunning intro video, as well as team portraits and countless dinner party photos. Nate Poekert, for shooting me in my kitchen—and around Nolita—and for managing to make me not look awkward ;) And my dear friend Christina Ware, who has worked hard to earn her title as The Yellow Table's biggest fan!

ABC Carpet & Home (and especially Shari Gab and Annie Bullock), for lending us plates, platters, bowls, glasses, utensils, boards, linens and just about every single prop we used in our food photo shoots. It was a dream come true getting to work with all of you.

PID Floors (and especially Pasquale Perpignano), for lending us hardwood floor samples each week for our photo shoots in exchange for cookies, cakes, and brownies!

Ashley Phillips, for offering valuable guidance throughout the cookbook process—and for volunteering to copy-edit! Sally Ekus, for graciously sharing your publishing expertise and encouragement. Lynn Carroll, at Worzalla, for patiently walking me through the daunting process of printing my first cookbook. Anne Willan, Joy Wilson, Sara Forte, and Julia Turshen, for your generous support of this book—your endorsements mean the world! And a big thanks to the lovely Olivia Funk for being such an enthusiastic and hard-working intern. Your help has been invaluable.

My over-the-top amazing recipe-testers: Alexis Ward, Cora Stuhr, Carrie Riggle, Munya Souaiaia, Jeannine Shannon, Gabrielle Griffith, Sylvie Gillard Cohen, Elizabeth Laurie, Hollyanne Fricke, Katie Crews, Megan Hartford, Alice Walter, Ginny Heidel, Sara Lenton, Christy Tenhaeff, Estephanía Lira, Olivia Wilcox, Erika Croonenberghs, Grace Rusch, Fawn Holsombeck, Natalie Race Whitaker, JC Carter, Maria Isabella, Julia Currie, Mary Beth Hunt, Jennifer Jackson, Caitlin Choi, Alyssa McClurg, Jin Lee, Christie Cady, Magdalena Szpara, Kirstin Frazell, Becky Lehmann & Emily Samuel, Jos Budge, Lori Hokeness, Rebecca Simpson, Jill Whitesell, Joella Chudy, Gail Hardie, Maude Humphris, Ginger Stark, Maria & Peter Larkins, Leslie & Kevin Chisnell, Courtney Delozier, Kris Clegg, Janey Ward, Heather Maclachlan, Christine Leonardo, Annie Middlebrooks, Cynthia Ross, Janelle Shank, Nikole Satelmajer, Annie Slocum, Nuria Seijas, Jackie Rice, Jacqueline Anderson, Bria Moore, Brita Britnell, Dana McQuaid, Melissa Auer, Elizabeth DeMaso, and Marne Duke. You guys did such an amazing job—not only testing the recipes, but throwing dinner parties and brunches as well. I am blown away!

My Kickstarter video team: Megan & Mike Gilger, for flying to NYC on short notice to shoot a gorgeous video, and for your amazing support of this project on every level. Tiago Veiga, for lending your mad editing skills. And to James Shortenhaus, for letting us use your fantastic song!

My road trip dinner party collaborators: (New York) Nathan Johnson, Drift Studio NYC, Belathée Photography; (Raleigh) Megan & Mike Gilger, Chris Heavener & Michelle Rider; (Nashville) Phillip & Dana Nappi, Heidi Ross, Ruthie Lindsey, Leigh Vail, Lisa Donovan, Handmade Studio TN, The House Nashville, Robin Riddell Jones, Evie Coates, Jamie Vick, Suzette Inman, David & Mae Ann Watson; (New Orleans) Joy Wilson, Rebecca Rebouché, Hannah McSwain; (Austin) Jeanine Donofrio & Jack Mathews; (Dallas) Sarah Harmeyer, Diane Brouillard, Kris Drayovitch, Samuel Melton, Jordan Strickler; (Los Angeles), Sarah Sherman Samuel & Rupert Samuel, Amy Dickerson; (Seattle), Jenn Elliott Blake, Sally & Chris Balt, and Elizabeth Rudge. Whole Foods Market for donating food and wine for the dinner parties, Volkswagen for lending a Beetle, and GoPro for providing a video camera.

All of my incredible Kickstarter donors, especially: Dori & Brian Friedman, Meredith & David Farhi, Pania Rose & Thaddeus O'Neill, Anna Richey, Hunter & Jill Whitesell, Lisa Vipond, James Muldoon, Christina M. Griffey, Elissa Rathe, Maggie Winterhof, Margaret Kincheloe, Maria & Peter Larkins, Phil & Christina Lee, Erin & Morriss Hurt, and Annie Middlebrooks. Your generosity is inspiring.

A super-duper thank you to Nancy & Kevin Race, and David Lawson, who went above and beyond to make this cookbook possible. I can't wait to cook each of you a fabulous dinner in the near future!

A huge thanks to my parents David & Mae Ann Watson, and to my brother Davis and sister Maria, for your unwavering love and support, for always encouraging me to pursue my dreams, and for being such huge cheerleaders of this project from Day 1. Also big hugs to my sweet in-laws Jim & Jan Carl, for your love, encouragement, and generosity. (I owe you all a truckload of granola!)

Lots of love and thanks to all of my Yellow Table blog readers for your amazing support, your comments, emails, and general awesomeness. I can't tell you how much it means to hear from you that you've cooked one of my recipes or thrown a dinner party because of The Yellow Table. This book is, in large part, for—and because of—you.

And most importantly of all, I want to thank my Lord and Savior Jesus Christ, who is able to do immeasurably more than all I could ever ask or imagine. This book is a testimony of His abundant faithfulness, and I hope that it is a source of inspiration and encouragement to many.

INDEX

(FOLLOWING PAGE) A few shots from the cookbook roadtrip!

CLOCKWISE, FROM LEFT-RIGHT: SAMUEL MELTON (1), MIKE GILGER (2,3), JACK MATHEWS & JEANINE DONOFRIO (4,5), MIKE GILGER (6), HANNAH MCSWAIN (7).

CREDITS:

All food in the book was shot on wooden floor samples from PID Floors (pidfloors.com).

ABC Carpet & Home (abchome.com) provided the tableware, cookware, and linens featured in the food photos, with the exception of a few privately owned pieces.

Wines in the book can be purchased through Le Dû's Wines (leduwines.com).

a dinner with

THE *Yellow* TABLE

{ AND LOVE & LEMONS }

tomato gazpacho
with avocado and mango

grilled skirt steak
with roasted red pepper
chimichurri

baby kale salad
with red cabbage, carrot,
avocado, and quinoa

peach blackberry crumble

#cookbookroadtrip